PRAISE FOR DANIEL QUINN'S *ISHMAEL*

"Wonderfully earnest and engaging. Think of Robert Pirsig in *Zen and the Art of Motorcycle Maintenance* or B. F. Skinner in *Walden Two*."
—*Los Angeles Times Book Review*

"A thoughtful, fearlessly low-key novel about the role of our species on the planet . . . laid out for us with an originality and a clarity that few would deny."
—*The New York Times Book Review*

"[Quinn] entrap[s] us in the dialogue itself, in the sweet and terrible lucidity of Ishmael's analysis of the human condition. . . . It was surely for this deep clear persuasiveness of argument that *Ishmael* was given its huge prize."
—*The Washington Post*

"As suspenseful, inventive and socially urgent as any fiction or nonfiction book you are likely to read this or any other year."
—*The Austin Chronicle*

"Deserves high marks as a serious—and all too rare—effort that is unflinchingly engaged with fundamental life-and-death concerns."
—*The Atlanta Journal and Constitution*

"The point remains that we are killing the earth along with ourselves and it is nearly too late to check our fate. This is reason enough for reading *Ishmael*."
—*The Orlando Sentinel*

Daniel Quinn

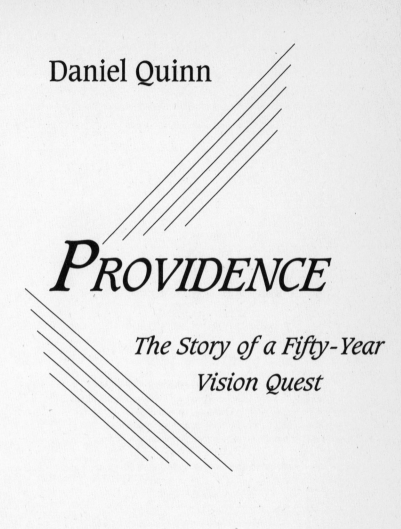

PROVIDENCE

The Story of a Fifty-Year Vision Quest

BANTAM BOOKS

NEW YORK TORONTO LONDON
SYDNEY AUCKLAND

PROVIDENCE

A Bantam Book
PUBLISHING HISTORY
Bantam hardcover edition / June 1995
Bantam trade edition / June 1996

BOOK DESIGN BY KATHRYN PARISE.

Library of Congress Catalog Card Number: 94-43423

ISBN 0-553-37549-0

Published simultaneously in the United States and Canada

Bantam Books are published by Bantam Books, a division of Bantam Doubleday Dell Publishing Group, Inc. Its trademark, consisting of the words "Bantam Books" and the portrayal of a rooster, is
Registered in U.S. Patent and Trademark Office and in other coun-
tries. Marca Registrada. Bantam Books, 1540 Broadway, New
York, New York 10036.

PRINTED IN THE UNITED STATES OF AMERICA

BVG 10 9 8 7 6 5 4 3 2

Only slaves love being powerful.
HANS ERICH NOSSACK

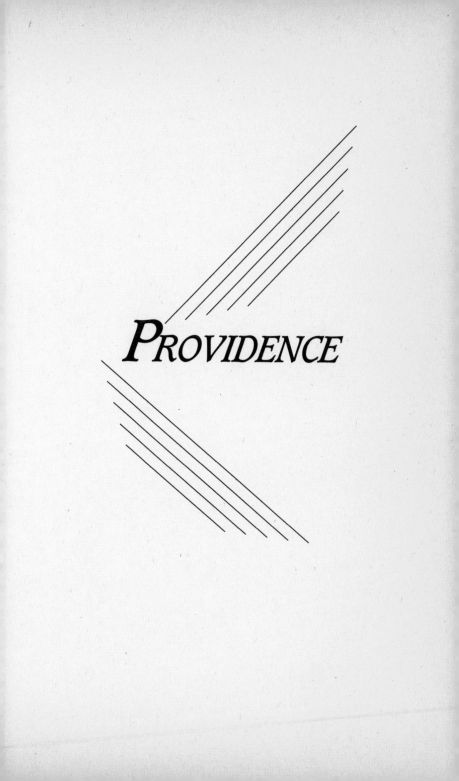

PROVIDENCE

ONE

Well, well, so, so. Yes, I'm awake. Awake now. Waking up. Give me a moment.

No, that's all right, really. No need to apologize, no need at all. It's true I was startled to see you here, momentarily startled, but . . . But you were—expected. I see this surprises you. I don't mean you in particular were expected, I'm not a clairvoyant. Someone was expected. Sometime.

In the middle of the night? Well, of course in the middle of the night! What better time? In the very dead of night!

No, we won't wake Rennie. She's a light sleeper, the lightest sleeper in the world, but the sound of people talking in another room nearby lulls her to sleep very nicely. Like distant surf, a babbling brook.

No, to tell the truth, I'm not really quite awake yet, but I'll get there. Another glass of tea. . . .

Oh, I know why you've come, you don't have to explain. You're welcome to explain if you like, of course, but you're not the first, after all. You're just the first to have the sense to break into my house at two o'clock in the morning!

You've come because *Ishmael* is a mysterious book. I can understand that. It *is* a mysterious book, even to me. You have questions about it and about me, and these questions aren't just expressions of curiosity. They touch on matters at the center of your life.

Let me start with something simple, a brief history of the writing of *Ishmael*. This will give us a sort of framework on which to build our conversation.

This is the way it was. Back in 1977 I had an idea for a book—or I imagined I did. I thought it would take me about six months, so I sat down and wrote it, and this was *Man and Alien*. But it wasn't quite all there, wasn't quite all together. In fact, it seemed to me that all I'd managed to do was to get a glimpse of the book I wanted to write. It was like a great unknown creature that crouched before me, facing away and blotting out the sky, and all I'd explored in this first version was the tip of its tail. That's all I'd managed to grab hold of. So I said, Well, I'll start over and get to the rest of it. It'll take me another six months. By then I'd fixed on one element of the book that was going to be explored again and again in every version thereafter, and this second version was called *The Genesis*

Transcript. Six months later I had a thousand pages of manuscript and I'd pulled myself up as far as the base of the tail. That was as far as I'd gotten in a thousand pages. So I said, Obviously this approach won't work; at this rate, the thing will be ten thousand pages long.

So I threw away the thousand pages, absolutely dumped them into the incinerator. Then I started the third version and worked on that for another few months, and this venture took me to the middle of the creature's back, at which point I once again said, Look, I can't get at it this way. I've got to have a whole new approach. So I threw that version away too. At this point we happened to have a small inheritance—a small inheritance that we in our simplicity thought was a very large inheritance—and I had a good idea of what I was going to do with version four, so we decided to move to New Mexico, to a whole new environment, and get this book done once and for all. So we moved to New Mexico and I tried something quite different for version four, and this was *The Book of Nahash*—*nahash* being the Hebrew word for *serpent,* the serpent that appeared in the Garden of Eden. So you see, I was still working away on that story. With *The Book of Nahash* I thought I'd very nearly done it, but this wasn't the case. I'd gotten up to the shoulder of the beast, but I still couldn't grasp what the damn thing was as a whole.

I said, Well, look, I don't know how to get to the end of this damn thing, so why don't I write a book *without* an end? That's what I tried next. I wrote *The Book of the Damned* and started publishing it in parts. I figured I'd just go on writing it and publishing it until I'd said everything I had to say. I produced three parts and they were in their own way more forceful than anything I've done since—but for some reason this method could only be pushed so far. I got to the end of part three and couldn't figure out how to proceed. *The Book of the Damned* had taken me up the neck of the beast and all the way to the crown of the head, but I knew I still had a way to go.

Now I began version six, which was *Another Story To Be In*. You can tell from the title that I'd gotten beyond the focus that had dominated versions two, three, and four. *Another Story To Be In* was a monumental effort, ultimately running to something like a hundred thousand words, but it was a success. In a sense, a success. For the first time, I had rounded the head of the beast and reached its snout. I had it in hand now and knew what the animal was at last. Everything was there—everything that would eventually find its way into *Ishmael,* and much more. I had no doubt that *Another Story* would be published (which shows how naive I was, even after twenty years in publishing), and I sent it off to one of the most powerful agents in the country with a light heart. Well, the agent hated it. He said, in effect, that the age for drivel like this had passed and that no one gave a damn about saving the world anymore. This was 1984, for God's sake, and Ronald Reagan was practically an object of worship in this country. My book was not only unpublishable, it was unrevisable. There was nothing—utterly nothing—that could be done with it. I should abandon it, trash it, forget it, and get on with my life. This is what the agent told me.

Well, I was pretty discouraged, I'll admit that. I knew he was wrong, but I also knew I needed a vacation from this book. I'd always felt I could do a horror novel if I wanted to, so I took out six months to see if I was right. I produced *Dreamer,* not a bad little book—just a diversion, of course, not a work of literature or anything. That pretty well exhausted my interest in genre writing. I published some stories and fooled around with a few other novels. Then at last I was ready to go back to work on *Another Story.* From a few years' distance, I could see that a lot of the agent's objections to the book were entirely valid. For one thing, as I've said, it was a hundred thousand words long. Amateurs imagine that publishers love huge books. This is true when it comes to authors with a following, like James Michener or Stephen King, but not otherwise. Readers aren't eager to spend thirty dollars for a book

> *The agent said that no one gave a damn about saving the world anymore. This was 1984, for God's sake.*

by an unknown author. Maybe they should be, but they're not.

And in truth there was a lot of cherished material in there that could be dispensed with, that was mere self-indulgence, so I went at it with a hatchet and cut the book in half. Then I sent query letters to fifteen or twenty publishers I thought might be receptive to its theme. Of course, I'm the world's worst salesman of his own work, I can assure you of that. I think three publishers asked to see it, and all three turned it down without a word.

As far as I could see, I was finished. I'd spent twelve years on this book. Not every minute of twelve years, but a good ten years of the twelve. All you can do is chase the deer, you know. You give it all you've got, and after that it's in the hands of the gods. If it's the deer's day to live, then it's your day to go hungry. I had to figure it was over, so I put the book away and got ready to hunt up a new direction for my life. And it was of course at that moment that I heard about the Turner competition.*

When I heard about this, I said, Well, okay, so it's not over after all. There was one more direction to try, and this was a good one. I heard Ted Turner talking. Everyone else was saying, Mr. Quinn, nobody's publishing stuff like this—nobody gives a damn. Turner was saying something different. He was saying, The human race is at risk here, and I'm not seeing anything new, not hearing anything new, and that's what I want to see. I want someone with some new ideas to come along and blow me away. That's worth half a million to me.

Well, of course that's exactly what I was all about. I'd spent a dozen years out there howling in the wilderness, and Ted Turner was saying, Well, how about it? Is there anybody out there who would like to be heard?

The only trick was, he wanted a novel. I'd always resisted writing it as a novel. I'd had the idea (wrong, as it turned out) that ideas embodied in fiction wouldn't be taken seriously by the reading public. But that was the deal, so I had to come up with version eight, and that was

---

* This competition, initiated by Ted Turner in 1989, called for works of fiction offering "creative and positive solutions to global problems." *Ishmael* was chosen from among 2500 entries worldwide by a distinguished panel of judges that included Ray Bradbury, Nadine Gordimer, Wallace Stegner, William Styron, and Peter Matthiessen.

Ishmael, and that was how I came to spend my thirteenth year on the book.

I didn't expect to win. I figured I'd be eliminated in the first reading, in fact, not because it wasn't what Turner was looking for but because it was *precisely* what he was looking for: something absolutely *new*—and therefore something that doesn't already have a slot in the matrix of *acceptable* ideas. I mean, after all, Turner wasn't going to be culling the entries personally. That was a chore that was going to be handled by a roomful of college grads who wouldn't know a valuable idea from a jar of Vaseline. That was my estimate, but I was wrong about that too— dead wrong. I'm told that *Ishmael* was recognized as the front-runner from the very first reading. For once in my life I was being more cynical than circumstances warranted.

At any rate, in May of 1991, when I learned that I'd won, this great beast that had been blocking my vision for so long was suddenly removed from my path by Ted Turner, who said to me, in effect, You don't have to worry about this anymore. It's finished. You no longer have to concentrate all your energies on figuring out how it can be done, because it's done. And as soon as this great body was taken out of my way, I saw that another stood beyond it, down the road. Not a "Son of *Ishmael*" exactly, but certainly a sequel in the sense that it *follows,* in the sense that it's a book along the same path. And that's what I've been struggling with ever since: that next book down the path.

TWO

No, don't apologize. I want you to ask questions, to interrupt with questions. That's your function here. You say you want to know what I mean by struggling, or why I've had to struggle. Let me think about that.

You can look at it this way. When people read *Ishmael,* it seems to them very simple, very obvious. And it seems like a work that must have been produced with no effort at all. That's good, of course. That's the way it should be. The reader should never see you sweat.

Here's a thing I never say: There are *new ideas* in *Ishmael.* Fortunately, other people say it for me. I was meeting with some group or other a few months ago—it was some folks from Greenpeace, actually—and a woman was trying to explain the book to the ones who hadn't read it, and she said, "The amazing thing about this book is that there are *new ideas* in it. Things you've never seen before, never heard before."

Just after the award was announced, I read a review of the book somewhere—a review written in advance of reading, you understand, a review written by someone who hadn't read the book—and this person said, "Well, look, we know there can't be anything new in this book, because everything has been said that is possible to say. There is nothing new under the sun." And I thought, Wow, I wonder when that happened? When was the very last new idea produced? Was it 1647, or 1763, or what? And how did they know it was the last one? Did all the thinkers of the world gather round and say, "Golly, there it is, the very last new idea in existence. From this point onward, all we can do is hash over the old ones."

Well, of course this is nonsense. Human thought didn't come to a standstill with Freud and Kant and Darwin any more than it did with Plato and Aristotle.

In *Ishmael* I cross over into virgin territory here and there. And these small incursions into the unknown were what cost me the years, with *Ishmael*. These small innovations were the product of years of struggle, and yet when you come across them in *Ishmael* people blink and say, "Oh yes! How obvious! Why didn't I think of that? It was right in front of my nose!"

Quite a few people have written to say, "Boy, am I annoyed at you—you wrote my book!" Then they go on to explain how they'd been working on exactly the same brilliant ideas—except that their brilliant ideas in fact bear no resemblance to mine. For example, people will say, "Yes, that's what I've always said: The Fall was what happened when we became alienated from Nature." But I don't say anything remotely like that in *Ishmael*. The equation of the Fall with alienation from Nature is a dreary old Romantic cliché that has been around for at least two centuries. It's every generation's great new discovery. But your question was . . . the struggle.

When *Ishmael* was out of the way, I looked at what was standing there down the road and said, "Oh my God, I'm going to have to tell the truth." For a writer, telling the truth is the struggle. Telling lies is easy. Telling lies is writing a book that anyone could write. Do you see what I mean?

> **For a writer, telling the truth is the struggle. Telling lies is easy.**

Let me give you a quote, the best thing ever written for writers, or for artists of any kind. It comes from André Gide, and I give it to all my writing students:

> What another would have done as well as you, do not do it. What another would have said as well as you, do not say it, written as well as you, do not write it. Be faithful to that which exists nowhere but in yourself— and thus make yourself indispensable.

When I spent all those years struggling with the book that ultimately became *Ishmael*, I was being faithful to that which exists nowhere but in myself. No one on earth could have written that book but me, and that's what Gide meant by making oneself indispensable. I wasn't making myself indispensable when I wrote *Dreamer*. Any competent craftsman could have written that. Not so with *Ishmael*. Only I could have written that.

When I looked down the road beyond *Ishmael,* I saw that I wasn't going to be let off the hook. I wasn't going to be allowed to write another *Dreamer*. I was going to have to go on being faithful to that which exists nowhere but in myself.

I understand what you're saying. You still don't see where the struggle comes in. Okay. Watch. Listen.

This is it.

You're seeing it. You're hearing it.

There are readers who love *Ishmael* who write to me to say, "I've read it four times," "I've given copies to everyone I know," "I'm going to be reading this book for the rest of my life." These are the readers who sense that there's something more to *Ishmael* than years of hard work and frustration. Over and over again, people ask, "Where did this book come from?" as if it were some very mysterious object. If I were to tell them that it was handed to me by an alien from another galaxy, I think there are those who might believe me. This is how strange it seems to them. They have the feeling that the origins of *Ishmael* must be somehow magical, and they're right. I don't mean to suggest that I'm anyone extraordinary. The universe shaped you to come here tonight to elicit this story. The universe shaped me to be here tonight to tell it.

This is the other half of *Ishmael*. This is the part that many readers sense was left untold.

In responding to readers' letters, I soon realized that the question "Where did this book come from?" doesn't have just one answer. It has dozens, because *Ishmael* came from every part of my life. I saw that some of the answers could be found in 1975 and 1974. But then I saw that some of them could be found in 1967 and some of them could be found in 1963. And some of them could be found even before that, in 1953. Finally I realized that the real beginning of the book had to be traced back to 1941, to one of the earliest memories of my life, and that's where I'll start here tonight.

> *They have the feeling that the origins of* Ishmael *must be somehow magical, and they're right.*

Some patient biographer may discover that I'm setting this event in the wrong house or in the wrong year, but it's the event that counts, not the house or the year. What I remember was that we were living in Mrs. Gilogly's house on 32nd Street between Dodge and Farnum in Omaha, Nebraska. I don't suppose any remnant of this lifestyle survives today, but it worked very well in the era of the Great Depression. Mrs. Gilogly's was a huge old family residence that had been converted into a boarding house, which made for a very practical and economical way of life. We had the top floor, Mother, Father, Dennis (my older brother), and I, perhaps four or five rooms. I remember only a couple of the other residents, but I suppose there must have been half a dozen, all white-collar workers or university students. It worked out very well for my parents, who both worked, since Mrs. Gilogly provided a sort of ad hoc day care for me, who was the only really young person on the premises (my brother being seven years my elder).

My parents were probably considered very modern, not only because they both worked but because they were very permissive with their children. Frankly, I doubt if this proceeded from any kind of principle, modern or otherwise. Mother liked the nightlife, such as it was in Omaha, Nebraska, at that time in history. They would come home from work, have dinner in the communal dining room downstairs, get dressed, and go out for the evening, coming home long after I was asleep. I think their attitude was that, since they liked to do as they pleased, it was only reasonable for their children to do as they pleased as well. I know that, at the very least, at the age of six, I would on Saturday afternoons, all by myself, take myself off to the movies, a mile or so away. I was a solitary child, even at this age, I don't know why. I wasn't conscious of being shy or special; I wasn't conscious of being lonely. Until the event I'm leading up to, I wasn't conscious of being anything, as far as I remember.

One night in the spring of 1941 I had a dream. It was the middle of the night in Omaha, Nebraska, in this dream—truly the dead of night, every radio silent, every lamp dark, every car in its garage, every man, woman, and child in bed asleep. Only one human being was abroad in that dead of night, and it was me. I was trudging home after a movie, head down, one foot in front of the other, down the long, silent blocks, past the dark, silent houses.

Suddenly I found my path blocked. A tree had fallen across the sidewalk. This was strange, because the tree hadn't been there two hours before, when I passed by on my way to the movie theater. I say it was a tree, and it was, but it was a kind of dream tree. It was the essence of a tree, which is to say it was a tree trunk. If it had been an actual tree, I would have come up against a huge tangle of leaves and branches, and the heart of the tree, the trunk, would have been hidden and inaccessible inside that tangle, which means that what happened next wouldn't have happened at all.

One night in the spring of 1941 I had a dream.

A great black beetle came scurrying down the length of the trunk to confront me, and I shrank back, terrified. I was terrified because all insects terrified me at this age and because I was sure the beetle was going to blame me for what had happened to its home, which was this tree. But the beetle spoke up immediately to reassure me. It wasn't a matter of vocalization. He spoke in my mind.

"It's all right," the beetle said. "Don't be afraid, I'm not going to hurt you. I just want to talk to you."

I drew a little closer, fear giving way to curiosity. It isn't often that an adult actively seeks communication with a six-year-old—and this beetle was definitely an adult. It had an aura of great wisdom and authority.

It, he. I had the impression it was a he.

"This tree was my home," the beetle said. "Mine and others', of course. Squirrels, birds, and so on."

"I know," I said.

"We'll have to abandon it now, of course."

I said I was sorry it had fallen down.

"That's all right," he said. "As a matter of fact, it didn't just fall down. We felled it on purpose to block your path, so I could talk to you. There was no other way to do it."

I was dumbfounded, of course.

"It's really dark out tonight, isn't it?" he went on conversationally, making small talk to put a small boy at ease.

I said I guessed so, or something.

The beetle seemed to reflect for a bit. Then, conveying a feeling of great compassion: "You don't really belong here at all, do you."

I was surprised to hear him say this and asked what he meant.

"I mean, you don't really feel much at home in these streets, in these houses, in this world. You're not really cherished here."

Now that it had been put into words by this wise creature, I suddenly knew it was true. I felt tears stinging my eyes, as one does at moments of great revelation.

"The thing is," he went on very gently, "you're not *needed* here."

I nodded, unable to speak, too overcome with grief and with the great truth of what he was telling me.

"Well, well," he said, giving me a little time to recover. "But that's why I wanted to talk to you."

"It is?"

"Yes. Yes, it is. You see, you're needed somewhere else."

I blinked at him in astonishment and said, "I am?"

"Yes, you are. Very badly."

Once again I was dumbfounded. I opened my mouth but the word I wanted to utter wouldn't come out. It didn't matter; he knew what it was: *Where?*

"There," said the beetle, nodding toward my right. I turned and saw that the city lot beside me had vanished, along with its tall, dark house. In its place now stood a lovely forest that opened at the edge of the sidewalk, and I realized that the beetle's tree had come from this forest and not from the city lot. The fallen tree was a sort of bridge spanning the two locations, which were in reality hundreds or thousands of miles apart. About twenty yards away I saw a deer standing motionless in a little moonlit glade, watching me with grave speculation. Then after a few moments the deer turned and disappeared into a thicket beside him.

> *"We need to tell you the secret of our lives," the beetle said.*

"He wants you to follow him, of course," the beetle said. "We all do."

I tore my gaze away from the forest.

"We'll all be there, waiting for you," he went on, and then paused as if thinking about how to explain. "You need to know some things, you see, if you're going to help us. It will almost mean giving up your life, will almost mean becoming one of us." Then he added, rather shyly: "We need to tell you the secret of our lives."

I understood that he was talking about something that was meant to happen in the future, but I saw no reason to wait. I didn't want to wait and saw no reason to wait. The forest was there now, a step away, and I was entirely ready to give up my life to be in the company of these creatures, who needed me and wanted to share their secrets with me. In far less time than it takes to tell, I turned and stepped off the sidewalk—and was instantly awake. Instantly awake—and utterly heartbroken, sobbing uncontrollably until my mother came in to find out what was wrong.

"Did you have a bad dream?" she asked, taking me in her arms.

"No, no," I insisted. "It wasn't *bad*!"

She smiled at this. "Then why are you crying."

"I'm crying because—" But I was crying too hard to explain.

"Come on," my mother said, "tell me why you're crying."

"I'm crying because," I finally managed to squeeze out between gasps and sobs, "because—because it was so *beautiful*!"

I hadn't realized till tonight that the basic story framework of *Ishmael* is clearly derived from this dream, a fact I find quite amazing. In dream and in *Ishmael* an obstacle is laid across the narrator's path—in the one the trunk of a tree, in the other an ad in a newspaper (which of course arrives rolled up like the trunk of a tree). In dream and in *Ishmael* the narrator is confronted by a dark, threatening creature who immediately sets out to reassure him with words spoken directly into his mind. Both creatures, bug and gorilla, are "not where they belong"—have thrust themselves into an urban habitat in order to encounter the narrator. Both creatures come to the narrator from a habitat that has been destroyed. Both speak to the narrator as representatives of a larger community, a community consisting of all nonhuman life. Both tell him this community is in need of help—and that this help can only come from someone privy to secrets unknown to his fellow humans. Both invite him to take a journey of discovery that will alienate him from his human family and friends.

The purpose of the dream was to plant in me a lifelong yearning for its fulfillment.

Having had it pointed out to you in this way, you would be forgiven for thinking that I must have deliberately patterned *Ishmael* on this dream—or must at least have been aware of the similarities between them. I assure you that neither is the case.

What the similarities indicate, I think, is how deeply I accepted this six-year-old's dream as a description of my destiny. From that age, I knew that, somehow or other, I would make the dream come true—or rather, that I would finish it. I hadn't been allowed to finish it as a child —and this is exactly how I understood it at the time. I knew that its fulfillment was something that was to happen later. The purpose of the dream was to plant in me a lifelong yearning for its fulfillment. Someday I would be allowed to step off that sidewalk and enter another world.

That someday finally arrived when the hero of my novel stepped off the sidewalk and entered the world of Ishmael.

So you see that, even though I was unaware of it at the time, I endowed the narrator of *Ishmael* with a destiny that had been given to me in a dream half a century before.

THREE

Of course people don't think about destinies all the time—especially not six-year-old boys. I forgot the dream. Forgot it and remembered it—forgot it, remembered it, forgot it, remembered it—never forgot it.

Over the next ten years, the beetle's words took on new meanings. Something was going on between my parents. I didn't have any idea what it was and still don't.

On my birth certificate, my father, Herbert John Quinn—known as Bert and later as Q—listed his occupation as "Telegrapher" and his employer as E. J. Barrick, a successful Omaha roofer. Why would a roofer need a telegrapher? He needed a telegrapher because he had a curious sideline: He operated a sports book. This meant he needed a "line," which was both a telegraphic line and an array of sporting information of all kinds but principally the betting odds and point-spreads on offer for all the events of the day.

When Bert went to work for E. J. Barrick, he found his true vocation. I don't mean he became a bookie; that was some years in the future. The bookie is the man whose money is at risk, and Dad had no money to risk at this time; he was just an employee. He manned the phones, took the bets, kept the books, and played the subtle mathematical game that, if skillfully played, makes it unlikely that the bookie will ever have a losing week, no matter what happens. Ideally, the bookie makes money on every event, whichever side wins. Bert was good at the game.

In the early years, the office was just across the state line, in Iowa. I don't doubt that my father was on friendly terms with the famous gangster Meyer Lansky, who at this time was involved with the Dodge Park Kennel Club in Council Bluffs. Moving in the same circles, frequenting the same carpet joints, and making payoffs to the same officials, they could hardly have missed each other for very long; both intelligent, businesslike, and temperate, they would have had a natural affinity for each other.

Thelma, my mother, born Thelma Leona Warren, was also a telegrapher (she and Bert had met on the job in Florida) and brought in a second income through at least the early 1940s. Why she quit working I don't know, but, as I reconstruct these events now, this seems to have been the beginning of all our troubles. With endless amounts of time on her hands, Thelma became an obsessive housecleaner. She would literally spend ten or twelve hours a day cleaning a small apartment, then get up the next morning and start all over again at nine. She scrubbed the carpet twice a week with soap and water, on her hands and knees. She washed the walls once a week without fail. She vacuumed the floor and all the furniture twice a day, maybe even three times a day. She didn't even bother to put the vacuum cleaner away between sweeps. She washed the windows every day, every single one of them, and every mirror. She scrubbed the kitchen and bathroom floors every day. When we lived in a house, she would sweep the walks twice a day, always going far past the lot line; she would even sweep the street, if she thought it needed it. What most people would consider a spring-cleaning she performed every single day, seven days a week. Christmas was no exception, though she let us open the presents before she started.

I don't doubt that my father was on friendly terms with the famous gangster Meyer Lansky.

It didn't have anything to do with cleanliness, of course. Nothing was exactly clean. You could run a fingernail along the woodwork and scrape up a long curl of dirty, dried soap. She scoured the paint off the walls, pulverized the carpets, beat the furniture to death.

For the first few years of it, of course, I had no idea that this was odd behavior. Bert gave no indication that it was odd either but clearly found it maddening. He'd come home at six o'clock expecting dinner to be ready. Instead, Thelma was just finishing the bathroom and then had to vacuum the entire house. Nothing on earth could stop

her. By seven o'clock he was in a towering rage. By eight
o'clock they were locked in a terrifying, hysterical conflict.
This happened every night, or four or five nights a week.
Every night at six Bert would come home expecting dinner to be ready, though it never was. Even I, a child,
knew it would not be ready, that it could not ever be
ready, because ten hours was not nearly long enough to
finish cleaning our incredibly dirty house, which had to be
accomplished before dinner could be served. I couldn't
understand why he never learned, why he was unable to
reconcile himself to a process that could no more be hur-
ried than the setting of the sun or the changing of the
seasons.

My brother, seven years older, was by now in high
school and seemed to have a life of his own, apart from
the three of us. There was no one on hand to explain to
me (even if I could have understood) that my parents had
achieved a marital dynamic that worked perfectly for
them. Against all appearances, they were not on the verge
of breaking up. Chaos and conflict were as welcome to
them as peace and harmony might be to another couple. I
imagined that any day our family would be torn apart—I
even wished for it to be torn apart. In fact, as I much later
realized, nothing could have parted them; they were in-
separable in their antagonism.

It was Thelma who set the stage and created the premises for their battles. Bert didn't care where he lived. He'd
have been content to live in the same rooms forever.
Thelma, accordingly, was forever agitating to move somewhere that would be "less work." This was unanswerable,
of course. The theory was that if Thelma had "less work"

to do, we might be able to live "a normal life" (which is what Bert wanted, wasn't it?), so we moved every year or so, though naturally none of our new homes was ever "less work," so there was always cause to move again. Bert got tired of taking Thelma out drinking after their nightly battles, so she took to going out alone and coming home falling-down drunk —a new source of conflict. He gave up drinking entirely; she therefore took up drinking during the day—another new source of conflict. Mother was adaptable; if Bert had taken up sin, she would have taken up religion.

Surrounded by forces utterly beyond their control, children automatically take up magic.

Between the endless moving, boozing, housecleaning, and brawling, it seemed to me that we lived in hell.

Surrounded by forces utterly beyond their control, children automatically take up magic. This is something that doesn't need to be explained or thought about; it's as instinctive in humans as nest-building in birds. In its simplest, truest form, magic is performed as a demonstration, to show the universe what's expected of it. If you want it to rain, for example, you go out and sprinkle things with water. If you want it to stop raining, on the other hand, you make a fire and start drying things out.

The condition around me was this: Neither one of my parents seemed capable of understanding what the other wanted or needed. Thelma couldn't seem to understand that "all Bert wanted" was a quiet life—to come home night after night to the same house, to a sober wife, to dinner on the table at six or six-thirty. But Bert was no better in this regard; he couldn't seem to understand that Thelma was incapable of doing what he wanted; she "needed" to clean the house for ten or twelve hours every day and therefore "couldn't" have dinner on the table before eight or nine o'clock—or even ten o'clock on especially difficult days, when she might, for example, decide to repaint the bathroom or the kitchen, without neglecting a single one of her other, more usual chores.

Neither of them could see things from the other's point of view—but *I* could. This was evident. *I* understood what Father wanted from life. If I'd been my mother, I would have had the housework done by five o'clock without fail. I would have had dinner ready by six. On the other hand, I also understood what Mother wanted from life, and if I'd been my father I wouldn't have expected her to have dinner on the table at six or seven. I wouldn't have gotten angry if she'd gone on working till nine or ten or even midnight. No way. If I'd been my father, I would have been a perfect husband, seeing everything from Thelma's point of view, and if I'd been my mother, I would have been a perfect wife, seeing everything from Bert's point of view.

But of course I couldn't be them or force them to behave the way I wanted them to. I was in the same relation to them as the ancient rainmaker was to the elements. All I could do was produce in myself the effects I wanted my parents to manifest. All I could do was make myself perfect, the way I wanted them to be.

That then was my magic, to be perfect. It didn't work, of course, but no one in the whole history of the world ever quit on magic just because it didn't work. Nobody in the whole history of the world ever quit on *anything* just because it didn't work— magic, science, politics, love, religion. But especially magic. To give up on magic because it doesn't work would be silly. If it doesn't work, that just means you didn't do it right. That's how you *tell* you didn't do it right—when it doesn't work.

> *My magic didn't work, of course, but no one in the whole history of the world ever quit on magic just because it didn't work.*

Anyone knows that.

Of course, a perfect boy is an abomination, is an unnatural creature. The desired boy is the "real" boy, father to the desired "real" man, and by the time I was ten I was no longer anything like a "real" boy. In order to show the universe what was expected of it, I had made of myself an exquisitely delicate instrument, acutely sensitive to the feelings and wishes of others—and of course an exquisitely delicate and sensitive boy is nothing remotely like a real one. The people around me didn't like it—my own parents, teachers, other children, especially other boys. The girls didn't mind so much, because real boys of this age were generally not very agreeable companions.

I remember once visiting the house of a girl I was rather smitten with—or would have been smitten with if

I'd dared to be. As I recall, she was quite the most beautiful child in the class. At any rate, while she was making some effort to entertain me, her older brother—older, perhaps, by a year or two at most—made an unwelcome appearance. Having looked me over, he disappeared briefly. On returning, he handed me something wrapped in toilet paper, which I solemnly accepted and unwrapped. It was a turd, which he had just then produced on purpose to present to me. The girl was mortified, which of course was the object of the exercise. I was stunned, speechless. This was the act of a real boy, and we both knew it.

As things got worse for me, I got better—purer, nobler, more sensitive—which of course had the effect of making things even worse. By the middle of high school, everyone knew I was queer, meaning homosexual. I say "everyone knew," but I was the exception. I had no inkling of such a thing. These were

> *The desired boy is the "real" boy, father to the desired "real" man, and by the time I was ten I was no longer anything like a "real" boy.*

still the dark ages, and I was exceptionally naive. It had never occurred to me that persons of the same gender could be sexually attracted to one another. The idea would have astonished and appalled me. I was in fact attracted to nothing but girls, then or ever.

I remember my father once introducing me to one of his business acquaintances. "This is Daniel," he said, adding dryly, "he's a little *queer*." I knew he was getting at *something* but didn't have the slightest idea what it was.

I have to assume that there were boys inclined toward homosexuality at Creighton Prep at that time—why wouldn't there be? If so, they had the very good sense to act like real boys and stayed well away from me, knowing that not only was I not a real boy, I wasn't even a real queer.

It wasn't till I reached the wider world of the university that I began to understand the assumptions that were being made about me by people like my father. Given my well-developed faculty for seeing things from other people's point of view, I naturally tended to credit them with a perspicacity beyond my own. In short, never having felt the slightest tug of desire for a person of my own sex, I began to be seriously worried that I might be a homosexual.

Yes. Yes, I see what you mean. It sounds quite absurd now. At the time, the fashionable theory was that one could be a *latent* homosexual. This was deeply troubling, because the whole notion of being a latent anything means you can never be sure *what* you are. If a heterosexual can be a latent homosexual, then a John Bircher can be a latent commie, a nun can be a latent whore, a minister can be a latent murderer, and a jazz virtuoso can be a latent rock 'n' roller. Experience becomes meaningless—becomes irrelevant as a measure of interior reality, because the feelings you actually feel might turn out to be less real than feelings you never felt in your life.

———

I mustn't leave out an especially charming, if brief, episode in my life of this period. The summer between my freshman and sophomore years at college I worked as a lookout at a bookie joint in downtown Omaha. This wasn't my father's establishment. Bert worked behind a three-inch-thick steel door in a cavernous bunker under a cigar store known as Baseball Headquarters. My bookie joint was a small operation up a flight of stairs and separated from the public and the police by nothing but a locked door with a window in it, which was my station.

There was no baloney about passwords. If people walked up the stairs, as they mostly did, then they were players, and I unlocked the door and let them in. If they *charged* up the stairs, then they were obviously cops, and I made them wait while all evidence of wrongdoing was disappeared—a practiced routine that occupied perhaps twenty seconds. Then I let them in and we all sat around playing gin rummy or solitaire till they got bored and went away.

> **The summer between my freshman and sophomore years at college I worked as a lookout at a bookie joint in downtown Omaha.**

The high point of the summer for me occurred one afternoon when the toilet-paper salesman made his quarterly appearance. After writing up the order, he paused at my station and asked what I was reading. Feeling rather smug, I gave him a look at it: Joseph Conrad's *Nostromo*. The toilet-paper salesman shook his head disdainfully and said that a bright youngster like me shouldn't be wasting his time on such lightweight reading as that. He tore a sheet out of his order book and gave me a list that included Kant's *Critique of Pure Reason,* Sartre's *Being and Nothingness,* and Keynes's *General Theory of Employment, Interest, and Money.*

A horseplayer by the name of Angie gave me the benefit of his life's experience in this useful principle:

You can beat a race, but you can't beat the races.

FOUR

In the Quinn household, notions of God and Heaven belonged to a generalized childhood fantasy that included Santa Claus, the Tooth Fairy, and the Easter Rabbit. Small children were taught to kneel down at bedtime and pray "Now I lay me down to sleep" because it was a cute and harmless "part of growing up." I suppose the presumption was that, at the appropriate time, such whimsies would uproot themselves and be left behind, like baby teeth. Religion was not avoided as a topic of conversation; it simply had no existence.

When I was eleven, however, it came to my attention that my brother was "having instruction" in the Roman Catholic faith. I don't recall that he encouraged me to look into it; encouragement wasn't necessary. As far as I was concerned, if he was doing it, it was clearly a thing to be done. Dennis joined the army before completing his instruction (or at least before sealing the matter with baptism), but I saw no reason to follow his example in this procrastination. I took instructions and was baptized before the beginning of eighth grade.

I couldn't possibly have known that Catholicism was the ideal and very worst choice of religion for a child predisposed to believe that making oneself perfect is tantamount to making oneself lovable. This isn't to say that Catholicism insists on perfection; but if *you* insist on perfection—hunger for perfection—indeed, want to lose yourself utterly in the pursuit of perfection—Catholicism is the religion for you. The Church can definitely show you how it's done.

By the third year of high school, I was not only a queer, I was something much worse: I was a *pious* queer.

I was of course responding to needs much deeper (and far more human) than I knew about. I was of no importance to my mother, despised by my father, and loathed by my peers—and knew of no way to change this. What I did know was how to make God love me; I was assured of this; this was guaranteed. Being God, you see, he really doesn't have any choice in the matter; if you love him, then he jolly well has to love you back, no matter how personally repellent you might be. This is all right there in the contract.

You're probably thinking this can't possibly have anything to do with *Ishmael*, but it does. Consider this. Although I didn't know the biblical story of Ishmael at this time—probably had never even heard the name—he had already become the model for my life. Abraham's son by Hagar, a serving girl, Ishmael, along with his mother, was driven out into the desert when Abraham's wife gave birth to Isaac in her old age. When my mother gave birth to another son in *her* old age, when I was thirteen, I too felt myself driven out into the desert. Hagar left her son to die under a bush, but he didn't perish there. The cries of the forsaken infant fell on deaf human ears, but they were heard by God, who intervened to save him, and this is the meaning of the name he was given: *God heard*.

> *At the age of sixteen, I was already Ishmael, howling in the desert, yearning to be heard by the One Who Hears.*

At the age of sixteen, I was already Ishmael, howling in the desert, yearning to be heard by the One Who Hears.

It was at this age that I came across *The Man Who Hated God*, not a typical piece of literature for a boy reading Latin and Greek in a Jesuit prep school. It's the biography of an American roughneck who grew up (if my memory is right) in the late decades of the nineteenth century, became converted to Roman Catholicism in his thirties, and then (doubtless much to the horror of his family) entered a Trappist monastery. Self-willed, impulsive, and stubborn, he seemed (and proved to be) an unlikely candidate for the contemplative life. Nonetheless, after sufferings I frankly no longer recall, he subdued his unruly nature, made his profession as a lay brother, and in a long life attained great holiness, on at least one occasion performing what appeared to many witnesses to be an undoubted miracle. (By rule or custom, I'm not sure which, the Cistercians never seek canonization for their members.)

If you know anything about the Trappist life, you'll understand why I was drawn to it. It represents no sort of compromise between the monastic ideal of a thousand years ago and the realities of contemporary life. It makes utterly no concessions to modern religious fashions. These are things I could understand and admire.

The notion of penance (which is certainly central to the Trappist life) has virtually disappeared from modern Christianity, except when trivialized as the little packets of Hail Marys and Our Fathers that priests dole out in the confessional. The notion of living a *life* of penance makes persons of a modern sensibility squirm, because they're almost entirely ignorant of the worldview to which it belonged. They imagine that the penitential life was basically about people beating themselves up for their sins—and that wasn't it at all.

Medieval Christianity embodied a fundamentally heroic vision of the universe, with the earth the prize contested by cosmic forces of good and evil. They knew the earth was only a speck—that didn't matter. It was the speck that God and Satan had chosen at the beginning of time to be their battlefield. This was no metaphor. A very real war was engaged everywhere, at every level of being. Devils and angels struggled unseen to win the human race into the service of one army or the other. Heretics were not merely purveyors of mistaken ideas; they were traitors, saboteurs—Satan's fifth columnists. And the monasteries

—the monasteries were not conceived of as places of re-treat or refuge in those days, not places in which to find tranquillity and joy. Quite the contrary, the monasteries were understood to be the first line of defense against the almost overwhelming power of Satan. The monasteries were strongholds, bastions, citadels manned by stalwarts who had embraced the warrior's life for God, who lived the way soldiers live on the front lines—literally sleeping in their clothes so as to be ready for service at a moment's notice, laboring without com-forts, sleeping little, obeying the commands of their superi-ors without reservation, hard-ening their wills against the

If you know anything about the Trappist life, you'll understand why I was drawn to it.

temptations of sloth and self-indulgence. It was perfectly all right for civilians to enjoy the comforts of home, fam-ily, and friends, but these were not for the monks. Monks were the shock troops, the Green Berets—disciplined and fit, though they took their exercises in study and prayer—and indeed penance—rather than in calisthenics and the martial arts. Their prayers and their atonements for the sins of mankind held the enemy at bay, kept Satan from overrunning the world.

Well, you can see that this is an entirely different vision of the monastic life than is known to the average layman, who thinks of the monk (or the nun) as someone who is simply "running away from life"—from what they per-ceive to be "real" life.

Did I embrace this worldview? You mean at the age of

sixteen? Yes, I think I did, though I would not have been able to articulate it as fully as this. This was what was meant by being a "serious" Catholic, and I was certainly one of those. A "serious" Catholic "really believes" that all this stuff matters—sin, grace, redemption, heaven and hell, God and Satan. I wasn't just serious, I was super-serious.

This was an enterprise that no one could— What?

Oh, the enterprise I mean is saving the world. Even then I was obsessed with saving the world, though it meant something completely different to me then, of course.

Where was I? I was saying I wasn't just serious, I was super-serious. I was like a superpatriot; naturally I wanted to be sent right into action. Being super-serious, I naturally wanted to join the absolute toughest, most demanding outfit I could find, and that was the Trappists. The Trappists were fighting right at the front. People like the Jesuits and Dominicans and Benedictines were so far behind the lines they were practically civilians.

Of course at the age of sixteen this was something for the future. For the indefinite future. . . .

I'd have to say that from the age of twelve or so it was a settled thing in my mind that I was going to be an artist of one kind or another. This was because being an artist was like being perfect and like loving God: something I could do all by myself, without outside help. Do you see what I'm saying? I knew I couldn't succeed at something that required me to be *liked*, but I could succeed as an artist whether anyone liked me or not. I'm speaking now of the way a twelve-year-old understands such things. Artists can just sit in their garrets all by themselves and write or paint. No one can stop them, and if they're good at what they do, then they're good.

How is this like loving God? Well, you see, no one can stop you at that either. You can just sit there burning with love for God, and he's got to love you back, and that's that. You don't need to depend on anyone's *support* to succeed at being holy—or to succeed at being an artist. It's all up to you, all in your hands.

I was drawn to the arts for the same reason I was drawn to piety, because I could be good at them even if I wasn't good at anything else.

I don't mean to suggest that I could have verbalized all this as a child. It's simply my present estimate that I was drawn to the arts for the same reason I was drawn to piety, because I could be good at them even if I wasn't good at anything else.

I started taking private art lessons when I was ten or so. Luckily, I wasn't tremendously encouraged in this. I did a lot of painting in the next twenty or thirty years, but I was never going to be anything more than good.

Yes, that's right, the paintings on the walls are mine. I agree, they're good. I wouldn't hang them if they weren't, but look, there are eighteen million starving painters out there who are good, and most of them are better than I ever would have been. . . . These are all quite old. I haven't done any painting in fifteen years.

This is because when I paint, I paint, and when I write, I write. I couldn't do both. I had to choose one or the other, and I chose writing. I began to experiment with writing when I was in my mid-teens. It's no surprise that I found language a more satisfying medium than paint. Paint is unruly stuff, you know, not the best material for achieving perfection, whereas language does exactly what you want it to, no more and no less. If you want an elephant in a story, you say, "There was an elephant standing in the garden," and by God there it is—in three seconds flat—trunk, tail, ears, and everything, perfectly proportioned, exactly the right color and texture, every muscle and sinew in precisely the right place. Try to duplicate that feat with a brush and paint!

Like most people then and today, I lacked any clear idea about what writers are and what writers do. Obviously they fill pages with words, and they do this in such a way that people want to buy and read their books. Even this apparently naive and superficial statement reflects more understanding than I actually had. Writers, as I imagined them, sat in their rooms and were impelled or inspired to fill pages with words. Publishers, on learning that this activity had taken place, would then say to them, "You know, if these pages were done up into a book, people would want to read it."

"What good news that is," the author would reply. "How fortunate it is that there is some correspondence between what I am impelled or inspired to write and what the general public likes to read!"

As the time drew near for me to give serious thought to my adult career (always provided I didn't become a Trappist monk), I decided that winning the esteem of the world by filling pages with words would suit me very well. At this time, the best known and most admired authors in America were William Faulkner and Ernest Hemingway. I read their work and found it not too difficult to fill up pages of my own that seemed very similar to theirs. I sent a collection of these pages to the Writers' Institute at St. Louis University, and they replied by awarding me a full scholarship.

Like most people then and today, I lacked any clear idea about what writers are and what writers do.

Nowadays it seems to be fairly well understood that writers know something about writing that English teachers don't. In 1953, however, this apparently wasn't even guessed at, for there wasn't a single writer on the faculty of the Writers' Institute. As a result, when we aspiring writers handed in stories, they didn't come back with comments like "Nicely written, but no one on earth will publish it." They came back with the same comments we'd had from our high school English teachers, comments like "Very good" and "Interesting idea." In our classes, to the best of my recollection, no one ever talked about what was involved in getting published. It seemed to be taken for granted that if we were "good enough," publication would surely follow and was not something that could otherwise be usefully thought about.

To be fair to the faculty, I gave the program only two years. To be fair to me, in two years I didn't acquire a single new skill or a single new understanding that would be relevant to a writing career. I don't mean to suggest that I was outraged by this failure. I was, after all, only marking time until I could take up my true vocation, which was to the religious life. It seemed to me now, though, that I'd waited long enough, that I'd given the idea long enough to go away if it was going to go away, and it hadn't. I still wanted to become a Trappist monk. . . .

Yes, that's a valid point. I'm expressing this as I perceive it now. Naturally, when I was twenty years old, I spoke in terms of "having a vocation," but this didn't presuppose that I'd received a personal summons from God. If you felt an attraction to the religious life, this was assumed to be a reasonable indication that you had a vocation.

On the subject of attraction and assumptions . . . it's often assumed that my attraction to the Trappist life must have been inspired by Thomas Merton. After the appearance of *The Seven Storey Mountain*, he'd become the world's most renowned Trappist as well as one of the world's most renowned religious writers, but I wasn't going into the Trappists to pursue the intellectual life or to become a writer. Merton was far less what I had in mind as a model than that roughneck cowboy of *The Man Who Hated God*. Although I made my application for admission to Our Lady of Gethsemani in Kentucky, where Merton lived, I had no reason to suppose that I'd ever meet him or exchange a syllable of conversation with him. In fact, I wasn't particularly asking to be admitted at Gethsemani and said in my letter that I'd gladly go wherever I was told to go. At that time the Trappists had several U.S. foundations.

As it happened, however, Merton was at that time the novice master at Gethsemani, which meant that it was he who received my letter and he who decided there was no reason why I should go anywhere else. . . .

I'm smiling because when I say "as it happened," I really mean "as Providence would have it." If I'd written to a different monastery, if someone other than Merton had been the novice master, or if he'd sent me to a different monastery, my whole subsequent life might well have been quite astonishingly different.

> *It seemed to me now, though, that I'd waited long enough. I still wanted to become a Trappist monk.*

Yes . . . my family. I remember my mother making the expected speech about "throwing my life away," and what terrible thing had I ever done that I needed to go and do penance at a monastery? I don't recall my father's reaction; I can't think he would have been much surprised. After all, I'd always been a queer boy, in every sense. . . .

That's an acute observation. I don't remember their reactions very well because they were no longer deeply involved in my life or I in theirs. I'd given up on them, you see. They were clearly hopeless, still tearing and rending each other like a couple of savages, and my being perfect had been completely wasted on them. But now I had another use for perfection. Now I could be perfect for someone who *appreciated* perfection, who knew the *value* of perfection—indeed for someone who had said in so many words, "Be perfect, as your heavenly father is perfect."

That too is an interesting observation. I *do* sound as if I despise this boy, who was having so much difficulty becoming a *real* boy. Let me think about that. . . .

I don't think I despise him, in fact I'm quite sure I don't. It's simply that I'm allowed to laugh at him. I'm allowed to laugh at him and at his very painful adolescence, because, after all, he was me. I wouldn't take it kindly if *you* were to laugh at him, however. You don't know him well enough for that.

Now where was I? I guess I was on my way to the monastery. I got there somehow, but, for all I remember, it might have been by bicycle.

FIVE

People of modern sensibility can admire someone who enters a religious order to do good works of some kind, to teach or tend the sick or feed the poor. Even sanctity can be swallowed if it's a good, healthy, *active* kind of sanctity, like Mother Teresa's. What people don't like to see nowadays are saints skulking in their cells staring glassy-eyed at a crucifix. This sort of sanctity strikes them as morbid and sickly, and naturally this was exactly the sort of sanctity I had in mind for myself.

In my school career, all my efforts had gone into demonstrating that I was a genius. If I was a genius, then it didn't matter if I was queer. Or, perhaps more accurately, if I was a genius then being queer was okay, because all geniuses are queer, aren't they? But I wasn't entering the monastery to continue this career. I didn't need or want to demonstrate my brilliance. I wanted to be shed of all that. I didn't want to shine, I wanted to become nothing, to be enfolded in the Lord, and disappear.

No, no, here I'm speaking the literal truth. Hold on, I'll be back in a minute. . . .

This is a poem I wrote a few months before I left for the monastery. It's called "The Old Acolyte's Easter."

They found me hidden in a dark corner.
The candles had dissolved to pools, and they,
Finding themselves in darkness, looked for me,
I being the candle-lighter. And so they found
My bones hidden in this dark corner, and they
Rejoiced with me that I had been discovered—
And not only I, but my bones. They gathered me up
Easily, for, hiding there, I had become a web,
Clinging to the walls as I petrified, and when
They touched me I gave no resistance but loosened
Even this mild grip and fell into their hands.

This is what I had in mind for myself, self-effacement to such a degree that I could die and not be missed.

Apparently you find this puzzling. I'm not sure why. . . .

Ah, yes, I see, that's a good point. When I thought of myself as a writer, the objective was entirely different. As a writer, I wanted to stand in the spotlight of public attention and adulation, there's no doubt of that. These were the two forks in the road ahead of me, and each had its attractions. I could go either way, toward what I imagined would be fame and glamour and fortune or toward complete poverty and anonymity. It had to be one extreme or the other. The middle of the road has never had any attraction for me.

In my fantasy of monastic life, I would on arrival, as the newest newcomer, be given the humblest chores to do, and I would do them—to perfection, of course. Naturally my fantasies didn't run to cleaning latrines or washing dishes. I thought in terms of scrubbing floors. There I'd be, lost in meditation, scrubbing away for hours on end but oblivious of the passage of time. In ten or twenty years I could work my way up to being the candle-lighter of my poem.

> *I didn't want to shine, I wanted to become nothing, to be enfolded in the Lord, and disappear.*

Of course the actuality was nothing at all like this. The novices were rather like a special class at a school, and I was received by them like a new classmate. I was immediately assigned a guardian angel (literally so-called), a novice my own age, whose job was to see that I had everything I needed and got everywhere I needed to be. I remember this handsome and good-natured young man very vividly. I'm sure he must have been the prom king at his high school and the valedictorian and probably the captain of the football team.

Something I couldn't possibly have anticipated happened: I was *accepted* by this group. I was welcomed and made to feel . . . worthy. I was completely bowled over by it. Nothing like this had ever happened to me. I wasn't on trial. I didn't have to prove myself. Thinking about this now, I realize that for the first time since early childhood, I didn't have to prove that I was a real boy or a real man. There was utterly no machismo here. Gethsemani wasn't about manhood, it was about sainthood.

Decades later I realized that the silence saved me. I assume you know that, among the Trappists, you speak only to your spiritual director or confessor. There's a rudimentary sign language—deliberately rudimentary—but this is for necessary communications, not for idle chitchat, at least in theory.

I say that silence saved me, because, growing up, from age ten to age twenty, language had been my weapon, virtually my only weapon. I wasn't strong or fast or big, wasn't physically aggressive, so I fought with my tongue. Made enemies with my tongue. This was all right too, because being shunned for viciousness is much easier to take than being shunned for queerness. But I walked into Gethsemani without a weapon of any kind, having denied myself speech. And, having denied myself speech, I was unable to make enemies—and, for the first time in a long, long time, *didn't* make enemies.

People without much imagination will say things like, "Oh, it must have been terrible for someone as verbal as you not to be able to talk!" Believe me, it was *heavenly* not to be able to talk—to have no one *expect* you to talk. To be honest, I didn't even much want to learn the sign language. I was perfectly content not to know what people around me were saying with their hands. It was none of my affair. If someone came up and told me the abbot wanted to see me, that was fine, I could make that out, what more did I need?

Merton lent me a copy of Max Picard's *The World of Silence*, a wonderful book, a whole book on silence, and nothing I could say in praise of silence could begin to equal it. Father Louis—that was Merton's name in religion—was a marvelous person, full of humor and charm, not in the least austere or self-important or solemn. What my guardian angel was to me, Father Louis was to the novices as a group, and he brought us along rather like a good-natured football coach. Not all the novices were youngsters. Two were ordained priests from other orders, one in his thirties, the other in his forties. He treated the rest of us—the ten or twelve youngsters—the same way he treated them, as if we were grown-ups worthy of his respect. Obviously he knew things about the contemplative life that we didn't know, couldn't even begin to guess, but he was just there to enlighten us and that was that.

I was far from being the only one who had arrived with romantic fantasies. One day Father Louis said—we had classes with him every day—"Look, you've got to understand that what we have here is a very *ordinary* life." Well, I think that drew a lot of smiles. Not many of us little saints were ready to believe that. He told us there were a lot of zombies walking around behind those beatific smiles we saw in the halls, and this certainly gave us something to think about, but no one imagined that something like that could ever happen to *us*.

Of course, it was all new and exciting to us, but what

Father Louis wanted us to see was that it wasn't always going to be new and exciting. It is, after all, a life of absolute regularity and unalterable, deadening routine, day after day, year after year, decade after decade—life utterly (and by design) without novelty. No vacations, no visits home, no days off, no cocktail hours, no parties, no scratch football games, no chess tournaments. In spite of that, a delightful merriment and glee flourished there that I've never encountered elsewhere. Holiness and reverence didn't preclude gaiety and humor.

Lightheartedness. That's what I found there: something almost unknown in today's world, crushed under leaden burdens of crime, crisis, hatred, and anguish. You should see the letters I receive every week from despairing teenagers. Who can live with a light heart while participating in a global slaughter that makes the Nazi holocaust look like a limbering-up exercise? We look back in horror at the millions of Germans who knew more or less exactly what was happening in the death camps and wonder what kind of monsters those people were. In fifty years our grandchildren (if any survive) will look back at the *billions* of us who knowingly and wantonly laid the entire world to waste and wonder what kind of monsters *we* were. . . .

One day while I was out weeding a tomato patch, an old horse-drawn manure cart went lumbering by. The younger of the two novice-priests was standing on top of the load and throwing out magnificent two-handed kisses to the world, just the way the pope does in St. Peter's Square. He was clowning, of course, but for whom? Not for us—I doubt if he knew anyone was watching and he certainly didn't care. He was clowning for God, displaying his thanks and his joy at being alive.

Was I happy there? Let's hold off on that one for a while. All questions of that sort will be answered in their place.

I should point out that I wasn't yet in the novitiate. I was a postulant—someone on probation, someone asking for admittance rather than someone admitted. That I was an outsider was plain from the fact that I still wore the clothes I'd arrived in.

As my spiritual director, Father Louis needed to know everything about me, and it wasn't long before he unearthed my literary ambitions. He wanted to see some of my work, and I wrote out from memory a few of my poems—including, I'm sure, the one I read you a few minutes ago. He looked at them and said, "Well, that's one thing settled: You're a poet."

> *Lightheartedness. That's what I found there: something almost unknown in today's world, crushed under leaden burdens of crime, crisis, and hatred.*

From his point of view, this wasn't something in my favor or something he saw as promising for my vocation. Just the opposite, in fact. As he had experienced it, the Trappist life was not congenial to the life of the mind. (I don't remember his words; this is what I understood from his words.) From ancient tradition, the Trappists are an order of peasants and laborers just as the Benedictines are an order of scholars and intellectuals. He told me very openly that he'd suffered in this environment—and wasn't at all convinced that I should go through the same experience.

I'll tell you something that may never have appeared in Merton's published journals. There came a time when, after months of anguish, he told his confessor that he was struggling with a temptation to write his autobiography. If it isn't already clear from what I've said, the writing of autobiographies is decidedly not on among the Trappists. But in this case, much to Father Louis's surprise, his confessor *ordered* him to write it. Thus, suddenly, it was no longer a temptation to be resisted but rather an obligation to be fulfilled, and time previously spent in more ordinary work was now to be devoted to writing. This was how *The Seven Storey Mountain* came about. . . .

Why did he tell me this? I don't know, I never wondered. I suppose it's because he was one writer talking to another. It's certainly something I would've done in his place.

SIX

Readers of Ishmael *often* assume that I must be a great lover of nature. Nothing could be further from the truth. I'm a great lover of the world, which is something quite different. Nature is a figment of the Romantic imagination, and a very insidious figment at that. There simply is no such thing as nature—in the sense of a realm of being from which humans can distinguish themselves. It just doesn't exist.

The nonhuman world? There's no such thing as a non-human world—not here and now at any rate. The world that we have is the world that has humans in it, just as the world that we have is the world that has air and water and insects and birds and reptiles in it. Every aspect of the world was changed by our appearance in it three million years ago, just as every aspect of the world was changed by the appearance of plant life three billion years ago. We've breathed in and out here for three million years, we've taken the substance of the world and made it into human flesh for three million years, and willy-nilly the world has taken that flesh back for three million years and redistributed it through the entire web of life on this planet.

Where would you draw a line between the human and nonhuman worlds? To which world does the wheat in our fields belong? If it belongs to the human world, what about the thousands of species that thrive in and around the wheat—and the tens of thousands of other species that thrive in and around them? It doesn't even make sense to say that this house belongs to the human world. Carpenter ants and termites are making a meal of it as we speak, I can assure you of that, and it would be a miracle if there weren't some moths in there snacking on our sweaters. The walls are inhabited by hundreds of different insects (most of which, thankfully, we never see), and funguses, molds, and bacteria flourish by the thousands on every surface.

No, it's nonsense to try to find two worlds here that can be separated into human and nonhuman. Biological and philosophical nonsense.

I'm not only not a lover of what is commonly called nature, I'm not even a lover of the outdoors. You can't see much of it right now, in the middle of the night, but there's a regular jungle right outside those windows.

Make your way through that jungle for about twenty feet —more or less straight down—and you'll come to a lovely little stream. I'm sure it's lovely, though I've never seen it. I've never traveled those twenty feet, and I doubt if I ever will. I bless the stream and wish it well. I don't need to see it to do that.

I give you this background so you can appreciate this fact: For my first three weeks at Gethsemani, I was kept inside. I mean I didn't set a foot outside for even a moment—and was completely content not to set a foot outside. It was a constant round of chapel, classroom, refectory, chapel, cell, chapel, classroom, refectory, chapel, cell. The weather may have conspired in this, I don't remember. I didn't even notice that I'd been indoors for three weeks, wasn't thinking about it at all, when one evening after we'd talked, Merton said, "I think it's time you went outside."

> *One evening Merton said, "I think it's time you went outside."*

I stared at him blankly. I'd practically forgotten that there was such a thing as outside. Father Louis explained that the next morning he and the novices would be going out to perform various chores, and I could come along and gather kindling.

Go out and gather kindling? What a marvelous idea! I, the non-nature-lover and nonoutdoorsman, was suddenly enchanted by the prospect of standing out under the open sky and breathing in the chilly spring air. Suddenly I was sick to death of books and walls, stale air and electric lights, hard floors and chairs. Suddenly I was overcome by a longing to hear wind in the trees, to see birds in the sky.

The next morning I woke up breathless, literally bursting with anticipation, though of course there were all sorts of things to get through first, like Mass and breakfast and our first class of the day. Finally, when the class was over, Father Louis came over and told me I could stay behind and read while he and the others went to change into work clothes. I'd be going out in my usual clothes, a sport coat and flannel trousers. . . .

Why didn't I change as well? Well, let me see. How to explain it? I didn't have any work clothes of my own to change into, and the others weren't changing into jeans or overalls or anything like that, they were changing into Trappist work clothes. In other words, they were exchanging an indoor religious costume for an outdoor religious costume, and since I was still a postulant, I couldn't join them in that.

Even so . . . ? Yes, that's an interesting question. Even if I wasn't changing clothes, what was the point of my staying behind? It's a good question. I guess the answer is that they had something else to do that didn't require my presence, because I know that at least half an hour passed while I sat there with my book. I have no idea what I was reading. I doubt if I was doing much reading anyway. I was too excited.

Finally my guardian angel appeared. I started to get up out of my chair, but he signaled me to stay put.

"We're going outside now," he signed. "Father Louis says you're to stay here and read."

"No, no!" I signed back frantically. I was frantic because I knew there was no way I could correct this misunderstanding. If I could have spoken, there would have been no problem. I would have said, "No, no, my dear fellow, you've definitely got it wrong. Father Louis told me quite distinctly yesterday that I was to go out with you today. It wasn't even my idea! He said, and I quote: 'I think it's time you went outside.' And just half an hour ago, at the end of class, he told me he'd send you to get me when it was time to go. Look, if you have the slightest doubt, just go back and ask him!"

But I couldn't convey anything as complicated or subtle as that. All I could manage with my hands was: "No, no, Father Louis say I go outside now!"

My angelic guardian angel smiled beatifically at my denseness, shook his handsome golden head, and repeated his message slowly and emphatically, as if to a child: "Father Louis says you're to stay here and read!" With that, he turned and scurried away.

My angelic guardian angel smiled beatifically at my denseness, shook his handsome golden head, and repeated his message slowly and emphatically, as if to a child: "Father Louis says you're to stay here and read!"

I was thunderstruck, completely crushed. Tears flooded my eyes. It wasn't just disappointment that overwhelmed me. In a single moment, the full realization of what lay in store for me in this life crashed in on me like a pulverizing boulder. I had been reduced to rubble, to nothing. Through a misunderstanding, of course!—but that was no consolation. On the contrary, that was the whole point! For the rest of my life I would be open to such misunderstandings at any moment. At any moment at all, it could happen that someone would walk up to me and deliver some ego-shattering command or message—even doing it with the kindest of intentions, just like my guardian angel. In fact, this encounter with my guardian angel was a perfect example of what the future held for me. This young man, moved by nothing but the sweetest benevolence, had walked in and obliterated me with a smile and a few gestures to which I was completely helpless to reply.

Yes, *helpless* was the word. I was embracing a whole lifetime of helplessness, of utter vulnerability. As I sat there alone in that bleak, empty classroom, my mind went dark with despair.

But of course I was under no *obligation* to embrace this life. I had no illusions on that score. If I wanted to, I could be back at my room in the dormitory at St. Louis University in a matter of hours—forty-eight hours, probably. There I'd find three of the only four close friends I'd ever had—Tom Anderson, Jerry Long, and Bob Cahill. They'd be delighted to have me back in their midst, there was no doubt about that. We would go and have a celebratory hamburger at the Kangaroo Room of the Melbourne Hotel just around the corner. Or dinner at Garavelli's, or a pizza and a few bottles of beer at Parenti's. We could pick up the conversation where we'd left off—not even a month ago!—Marshall McCluhan, Ezra Pound, the Symbolists, all the dark conundrums of modern literature that Walter J. Ong expounded in his classes, from which we departed in a state of intellectual meltdown.

Oh, that would be fine!

So the situation wasn't so desperate after all. If things didn't work out here at Gethsemani, I had an immediate alternative. In fact, a very attractive alternative. Of course, I had to give the Trappist life a fair trial, another month at least. It wouldn't be so bad. In fact, it *couldn't* be so bad, because as I went along I would know that I was leaving myself *a way out.*

It was at this point that I caught myself. What in the world was I *doing*? Because of a little disappointment—a very bitter disappointment, it's true —I was going to start living a lie. I was going to be behaving the same way as before, but now with an all-important in-terior difference: From mo-ment to moment I was going

> *No, I said to myself. You've got to choose, once and for all. Once and for all, finally, and forever. Or get out right now, today.*

to be holding out for myself the possibility of leaving. From now on I was going to spend every waking moment holding open my options: Well, if I can't stand this food, I can always leave. If I can't stand the way this teacher treats me, I can always leave. If I can't stand this kind of work, I can always leave. If I can't stand never having any time to myself, I can always leave. From this moment on it wasn't I who was going to be on trial, it was the monas-tic life!

No, I said to myself. You've got to choose, once and for all. Once and for all, finally, and forever. Or get out right now, today. Shut down those options absolutely or walk away. You came here to put your life in the hands of God *without reservation,* and what you're doing right now is establishing your reservations: I will live in the hands of God if everyone is nice to me. I will live in the hands of God if things go my way. I will live in the hands of God if people don't come around and tell me, "No, you *thought* you were going outside, but you're not." I will live in the hands of God so long as I receive no crushing blows to my sense of dignity and self-determination.

You know what it means to live in the hands of God, I said to myself. It means abandoning your will utterly. It means letting him direct the course of your life—even in this trivial matter of going outside—*without reservation.*

You've got to choose. Now. And not provisionally. Not temporarily. You can say yes or you can say no, but you've got to say one or the other.

Choose. Yes or no. Now, once and for all.

I summoned my will. I'd never done such a thing in my life before—and to be honest I've never done it since. Never had to do it.

I summoned my will. I brought it up like a deep breath taken underwater.

I summoned my will and held it like a deep breath taken underwater . . . and said yes.

Yes, now, once and for all. No reservations. No more daydreams about St. Louis. That was over forever, for me. I was *here.* Totally here, once and for all.

I released my will, and it flowed away, leaving me as limp as a drowned man.

And at that very moment my guardian angel swept into the room, his hands babbling apologies: I was right and he was wrong, Father Louis wanted me to go outside, so come on downstairs, we're just getting ready now!

I followed him on leaden legs, feeling nothing, not relief, not vindication, certainly not joy.

No, now that I think about it, it isn't right to say I was feeling nothing. I was feeling a sort of solemn terror. I was feeling doom. I had done what I had come to the monastery to do: I had given myself to God—without reservation—and now I was in for it, no matter what it was.

I followed my guardian angel down to a ground-floor room that had the scent and ambience—if not the sound— of a locker room before a big game. Drained and deeply depressed, I watched as the oth-

I went last, stepped over the threshold, turned around to close the door, then turned back to face the sunshine. And the god spoke.

ers finished manipulating themselves into the medieval equivalents of sweat socks and dungarees, with Father Louis in their midst exuding energy and high spirits like a benevolent trainer. It all meant nothing to me. I no longer cared where I went.

Finally, all their dressing done, the novices bunched up at the door and began to file out into the open air. As always, I was the last. This isn't a statement either of humility or of resentment. Wherever we went, no one followed me, because I didn't know the way. Everyone else knew the way, so naturally I went last.

I went last, stepped over the threshold, turned around to close the door, then turned back to face the sunshine.

And the god spoke.

SEVEN

I put it this way. I could put it other ways. I could say that, when I turned to face the sunshine, the veil that clouds our vision was gone from my eyes, and for the first time I saw the world as it is.

There are no words for it.

Someone blind from birth can't imagine what the sighted mean by color, can't fathom what this property might be. If all language were the product of a blind race, the word *color* would not exist, and if one of that blind race were suddenly to become sighted, he would be unable to describe what he saw; the words would simply not be there for him to use, and this is the way it is for me: The words are simply not there.

But I can put it other ways, and I will, because that's what I can do.

I turned and faced the sunshine, and the breath went out of me as if someone had punched me in the stomach. That was the effect of receiving this sight, of seeing the world as it is. I was astounded, bowled over, dumbfounded.

I could say that the world was transformed before my very eyes, but that wasn't it—and I knew that that wasn't it. The world hadn't been transformed at all; I was simply being allowed to see it the way it is *all the time*. I, not the world, had been transformed.

I'm trying. Be patient. We've reached the single most important hour of my life, and I have to get it right, have to come as close as I can to getting it right.

I gasped, literally gasped. I lost my breath, seeing that.

Everything was on fire.

I can say it that way, but when you say that something's on fire, you think of the fire as being *on* it—as a substance that is *on* the thing.

That wasn't it.

Everything was *burning*. Yes, that's better. *From within,* everything was burning.

Every blade of grass, every single leaf of every single tree was radiant, was blazing—incandescent with a raging power that was unmistakably divine.

I was overwhelmed. In a single second of this, of seeing this truth, tears flooded my eyes and poured down my face as I walked along behind the novices. It was strange to see fence posts sitting dead and silent and cold in the midst of this tremendous, thrumming effulgence.

In this vast, scintillating landscape, my nearsightedness was of no account at all. For as far as I could see, for hundreds of yards, thousands of yards, I could distinguish with absolute clarity each leaf, each blade of grass—no two alike anywhere. Each was crackling and trembling and all but exploding with the raging power that animated it.

Again I describe that power as *raging*. Look into a furnace blazing at its top capacity. Look into the heart of a nuclear reaction perhaps. The power that I saw thundering around me makes all our stock images of power seem feeble. But there was no violence or hatred in this rage. This was a rage of joy, of exuberance. This was creation's everlasting, silent hallelujah.

> **Everything was burning.** *Every blade of grass, every single leaf of every single tree was radiant, was blazing— incandescent with a raging power that was unmistakably divine.*

You know the sparklers they sell around July 4th. The world was ablaze with sparklers. Every blade of grass, every leaf of every tree was *charged* with energy—packed, jammed, evanescent with energy, which radiated forth into the air irresistibly. The whole landscape pulsed, breathed, moved, was made iridescent with this energy. I think, with what can be done in film today, I could produce a cinematic approximation of what I saw. It would be magnificent, but you would of course know it was just a trick. What I was seeing was *reality*, was the world as it actually is, every moment of every day. . . .

No, no, I wasn't in a trance. I wasn't in anything re-motely *like* a trance. I was gathering kindling, for God's sake! I had trailed the novices for awhile, walking through this madly radiant land, then had been signed to head off into the brush to get started. So there I was, stooping and picking up sticks, and breaking them across my knee or leaning them up against a rock to stamp them into smaller lengths, and making piles that would later be loaded into a cart, and all the while tears were pouring down my cheeks like a waterfall. It was lucky I was working alone, though I don't think I would have felt the least self-con-scious about my tears if there had been dozens around me. Who could have cared? Certainly not me.

It lasted for about an hour. The radiance just faded away, gradually subsided, and the world resumed its nor-mal appearance. The rest of the crew came along, and we loaded up the kindling and headed back.

Well, obviously that was the question: What did it mean? I would spend the next thirty years looking for an answer, and I want you to see how that answer developed.

This is how I understood it at the time: God had rati-fied the choice I'd made sitting in the classroom. God had said, "See? You made the right choice." It wasn't a re-ward, it was an affirmation. I had summoned my will and said yes to God, and God had summoned his will and said yes to me.

As I say, this is how I understood it at the time. It isn't the way I understand it now. Very far from it. . . .

Yes, naturally you want to know what I meant when I said, "And the god spoke." I'll get to it, believe me, as soon as I can, but I can't deal with it yet.

At the time, I dealt with it in the context I was operating in. I was a Christian pursuing the contemplative life, and there was a definite place in that context for the experience I'd had. God had made me a gift, a "free" gift, in that it hadn't been earned in any sense. It isn't possible to earn such a gift. In fact, in the literature of the mystical life, the gift has a name. It's called *infused contemplation*.

Now I had a problem. I had to tell Father Louis about this event—at least it seemed so to me. To keep it a secret from my spiritual director would have amounted to a sin of pride, would be to say, "Well, look, Father Louis, God and I have a few things going between us that you don't need to know about."

I had the rather naive notion that Father Louis would rejoice with me over this, so I didn't bother to think it through. I didn't try to anticipate his reactions, I just blurted it out. He listened for about ten seconds, then abruptly cut me off. My impression was that he was disgusted with me, disillusioned. Disappointed that I'd make something up like this in order to inflate my importance in his eyes. It was never mentioned again. . . .

Yes, I suppose I do feel somewhat bitter about this. He took it for granted that I'd made it up. There was no doubt of that. If he'd thought anything else—that I was mistaken or that I was psychotically deluded—he obviously would have wanted to know much more. By refusing to listen to what I was trying to say, he was clearly letting me know that he wasn't about to be taken in by some greenhorn postulant. . . .

Well, I understand what you're saying, but I see it differently. Father Louis wasn't a saint, wasn't perfect. As he would have said himself, the people in that monastery were very ordinary people, leading a very ordinary life. I didn't take that into account when I told him what had happened. I expected him to be perfect. I expected him to behave like a saint, and instead he behaved like an ordinary person. . . .

Yes, you're probably right: I still think he should have behaved like a saint. I would say rather that I *wish* he'd behaved like a saint. I trusted him, took a great risk with him, opened myself up to him, and he dismissed me as a fake. He gave me the kind of reply I would have expected from my father, not the kind of reply I expected from my spiritual director. It hurt me.

But it didn't matter as deeply that day as it would have the day before. I had said my yes. I was at Gethsemani to stay.

This marked the beginning of a new phase of life at Gethsemani, though it lasted only a very short time—a few days at most. I now went out every day with the novices. One day, as I mentioned earlier, we went out to weed a field of tomatoes. Another day, we went to the woodshed to split logs for firewood.

There I was in my Brooks Brothers sport coat and gray flannel trousers, swinging a mallet. After an hour or so, I was literally staggering with exhaustion and my hands were masses of broken blisters. I was completely out of shape, of course. The monk in charge of the operation—not Father Louis—came over and told me it was time for me to quit. I, the little saint, said, "No, no, I'm all right. I can go on." Two minutes later, I took a clumsy swing and broke the shaft of the mallet I was using.

I carried the pieces over to where the monk was standing and said, "I'm sorry. I broke my mallet."

"It isn't *your* mallet," he snapped. "It belongs to the *community*."

I tell this story to make the point that I was *learning* how to make enemies at the monastery. I had no idea how irksome I was being, playing the little saint, courageously and stupidly insisting on working when I was no longer competent to work, when I might easily have injured myself or someone else.

The monk was perfectly right to rebuke me. I was thinking of the mallet as mine. I was thinking of nothing but myself and how much I was suffering and how noble and heroic I was being, but I was completely unaware that this *showed*. I was in fact beginning to reveal my true colors; once people began giving me things to *do* I began to implement my fundamental psychological strategy: *If I'm perfect, people will love me.* I knew God wanted me to be perfect; Jesus himself had said so: "Be perfect as your Heavenly Father is perfect." I was certain that nothing is more lovable than perfection and had no inkling that nothing is more irritating.

It didn't matter.

A couple days after this episode, Father Louis called me

into the little cubbyhole he used as an office and told me
he had decided I should leave the monastery.

In an earlier conversation, Father Louis had revealed the
fact that he had only recently "discovered" Sigmund
Freud. He knew this was an oddity for someone who had
moved in sophisticated circles before entering the monastery, but he was perfectly open about it. He had missed
out on Freudian thought and was now making up for it.

One result of his newfound enthusiasm for Freud was
that he had instituted a rudimentary sort of psychological
screening of monastic candidates: Before admission, they
were to take a Rorschach test. He had just now, he told
me on this day, received the results of my test, which I'd
taken in Omaha a week before leaving for Kentucky. . . .

Why do I call it rudimentary? I don't mean the test is
rudimentary. I mean that using it as the sole measure of
someone's psychological status is rudimentary. Don't
misunderstand me: I'm not suggesting it was inadequate.
In my case, I'm sure it was more than adequate. Father
Louis didn't describe the results in detail, but it's not hard
to imagine what they were. I was a very insecure and
immature young man, terrified of sex, incompetent in
personal relations of almost every kind, full of self-doubts,
and desperately low in self-esteem, and the Rorschach
could hardly have missed all that.

What the Rorschach indicated, Father Louis said, keeping it simple, was that I had some growing up to do. I
said this struck me as unfair—everyone has some growing
up to do at age nineteen! He had little choice but to point

out that some nineteen-year-olds have more growing up to do than others.

When it became clear that the decision to send me home wasn't discussable, that I wasn't going to be given any chance to prove myself at all, I couldn't hide the depth of my disappointment. I wanted to, believe me, but there was no holding back the tears.

I was utterly crushed. I couldn't have been more wounded if Father Louis had taken out a hammer and hit me on the head. This was a rejection that went beyond any rejection I'd ever known. This was rejection not only by Father Louis, this was rejection by God himself.

Obviously this was the way I perceived it, not the way Father Louis presented it. He said something like this: "Look, I didn't ask to be the novice master—or even want to be the novice master—but the abbot asked me to take on this task. Providence has put the disposition of these things into his hands, so I had to conclude that this was what God wanted me to do at this time. A different abbot might have chosen a different novice master, but this abbot is the one we actually have, and he chose me. And because he chose me, the disposition of things pertaining to the novices is in my hands. In other words, Providence has put it into my hands to decide who comes to Gethsemani and who doesn't and to decide who stays at Gethsemani and who doesn't.

> *Father Louis called me into the little cubbyhole he used as an office and told me he had decided I should leave the monastery.*

"Another novice master might have made a different judgment in your case, but I'm the novice master you actually have, and this is what I judge to be the best thing for you right now. As your spiritual director, I think the best thing for you is to go back out into the world, and you can either shake your fist at the heavens for treating you unfairly or you can accept this as an act of Providence.

"I'm no more important in the divine scheme of things than you are. I was put here, first, to make sure that you *got* here and, second, to make sure that you didn't *stay* here. As far as I'm concerned, this is what God wanted for you. This says nothing about what he'll want for you in three years or five years or ten years. If God wants you to come back to Gethsemani, then that's fine. I'm not banishing you forever, I'm just sending you back out into the world to do a little more growing up."

I heard the words, I understood the words, but they couldn't wipe away my feelings of desolation and abandonment and humiliation. I asked him if I could at least stay till Easter, which was ten or twelve days away, but he didn't think that was a good idea. . . .

What? Of course I felt humiliated! My God, I hadn't even lasted a month! How was I going to explain this? Was I going to lie and say it was just too tough for me, or was I going to tell the truth and admit that I'd been chucked out? Those were the only explanations I could offer: Either I was a wimp or I was a sicko.

I'm sitting here wondering if I really need to go through the next two weeks, which were very painful indeed. I suppose I'd better. To leave them out would just be sparing myself. . . .

Merton's enthusiasm for Freudianism was rather like a convert's. He was sold on it and wanted everyone else to be sold on it. In a word, he thought I should immediately go into psychoanalysis, and he began to make plans for me to do this directly from the monastery. It's easy enough to see now that he was seriously overreaching when he took it upon himself to operate in this sphere, but I certainly didn't see it at the time. Psychoanalysis was all he knew about, so naturally it was his answer to every condition and situation. It didn't matter whether I was a borderline psychotic or just a kid who needed to do some growing up, I needed psychoanalysis. I didn't agree, but what did I know? This was my spiritual director, and to put myself in his hands was to put myself in the hands of God.

> *His enthusiasm for Freudianism was rather like a convert's. He thought I should immediately go into psychoanalysis whether I was a borderline psychotic or just a kid who needed to do some growing up.*

I moved over to the retreat house, a miserable, depressed exile. The days dragged past. Father Louis was bent on shuttling me directly to the Menninger Clinic in Topeka. As I say, what did I know? I was in a daze, grieving, stunned.

I remember one day he dropped by my room in the retreat house with the air of someone making an obligatory visit to death row. I was no longer fully among the living. One day the abbot stopped me in the hall, and I thought he was going to wish me well or to tell me he was sorry things hadn't worked out for me, but no, he just wanted to make sure I understood I couldn't use the monastery to hide from the draft; I had to get in touch with the Selective Service as soon as I got home. I told him I understood that, and he turned and walked away without another word.

When the next retreat broke up on Palm Sunday, I got a ride with one of the retreatants back to the airport. He was clearly eaten up with curiosity about me, about life inside the monastery, and of course especially about why I was leaving. I was not forthcoming. He said he guessed it must be a very tough life. I said, "Yeah."

That night I checked into a hotel in Topeka, Kansas. In the morning I reported to the clinic for a battery of tests, which I'm sure laid bare in new and wonderful ways everything I've told you and more. The high point came a couple days later, when one of the staff arrived with a clipboard to gouge out the sort of specifics that the tests couldn't provide. He knew the weak points and sore spots, knew where to probe for the terrors and doubts that I'd hidden from everyone.

I could have told him to get lost, but I didn't realize that. In my simpleminded fashion, I still imagined I was traveling under orders from God, and if God wanted this psychiatrist to invade my inner space, all I could do was submit. I submitted. He spent some two days tearing me apart to see what was festering inside.

Meanwhile my father was driving down from Omaha to collect me, and he was scheduled to arrive late in the afternoon of the second day. Naturally he was paying for all this, which made him the client. It was understood that the psychiatrist would make his report and his recommendations to Bert, then it would be over.

"But you're not going to tell my father all this stuff, all this stuff we've been talking about."

The psychiatrist assured me that he wasn't going to do that.

Well, of course he did. That almost goes without saying, doesn't it? He didn't hold back anything. The doctor knows best, after all, and, as I say, Dad was the client, not me. I just sat there like a drooling moron, my ears crimson, while he pumped it all out.

I can't imagine what we talked about in the car going home. Maybe we didn't talk at all. I thankfully have no memory at all of what happened next or of the weeks that followed.

EIGHT

Yes, that's certainly the question. How could I reconcile the hour of sight that I'd been given at Gethsemani with what followed? I couldn't. It simply didn't make any sense. Here's the way I was thinking about it: God wanted me to say yes to the monastic life, and then he kicked me out. It made no sense in those terms and still makes no sense in those terms. It took me thirty years of searching to find the terms in which it does make sense, and we'll get to that in its proper place in the story. . . .

No, I'd rather not give you any hints at this point. Well, I'll give you this one hint. I've avoided the word *vision* to describe what happened, because what I experienced was not "a vision" in the sense of . . . This was not a *Christian* vision. I didn't have a glimpse of heaven or of throngs of angels or of Jesus or Mary. There was simply nothing Christian about it. It was irrelevant to Christianity. Christ said, "My kingdom is not of this world," and for two thousand years everybody knew that he meant exactly what he said. What I saw that day was not His kingdom. Not, not, not, not, not. What I saw that day was the *world,* and Christ never made anything clearer than the fact that he was not of *this* world, he belonged to the world *above.*

At Menninger's they'd given me a choice of therapists from their list of Menninger-trained psychoanalysts all over the country, and I chose one in Chicago, because I had friends there—Jerry Long and Bob Cahill, who, like me, had given up on the Writers' Institute and were now at Loyola. I'd missed a semester by going to Gethsemani, and I decided to try to make up as much as I could at summer school, so, after a few weeks in Omaha, I headed to Chicago to find an apartment.

By this time I'd achieved some psychological distance from the ordeal. I'd had to stand off from the religious life, for safety's sake, because I no longer knew where I stood with God. It no longer made sense to invest too much of myself in His cause. Now, in order to rebuild my shattered self-esteem, I had to invest myself in something else, which was writing. I'd failed as a saint, but—

Yes, that's a good point. I said a few minutes ago that I'd imagined becoming a saint was simply a matter of choice, something you could either choose to do or not, because if you loved God, God had to love you back. This had proved to be not the case. But writing was different— presumably. Unlike becoming a saint, becoming a writer is something that's entirely in your hands. If you have the talent and the determination, you can do it. You don't need to be loved, you don't need to take a Rorschach test, you don't need anyone's permission. So this was how I planned to rebuild my self-esteem. Once again, I don't mean I figured this all out consciously. I mean that I had by now ceased to think of my future exclusively in terms of sanctity and had instead begun to think of it in terms of writing, and this is why.

Oh, you don't have to remind me, I'm not going to ne- glect that. I was supposed to be in Chicago because a certain psychoanalyst was there. This was Dr. Zirpoli— Robert, if my memory is correct. My relationship to him was false from the start. I couldn't have known it, but I'm surprised he didn't—or perhaps he did and considered it simply as a clinical problem to be solved. With the possi- ble exception of something like behavior modification (which is more a matter of retraining than of therapy in the classical sense), psychotherapy is useless for someone who thinks he's not in need of it. If I'd been honest, I would have said, "Look, Dr. Zirpoli, this is all a waste of time. There's nothing wrong with me, so it's stupid for me to sit here with you hour after hour, week after week." Now that I think about it, the chances are good that I actually *did* say something like this to him. Doubtless he replied by asking me why I didn't just walk out if I felt this way. See if you can guess how I would have answered him. . . .

No? I think you could if you tried.

I would have answered him this way: "The reason I don't walk out is that my spiritual director thought this is what I should do. I don't necessarily agree with his judgment, but it's not my place to gainsay it." This is what Dr. Zirpoli would have called (quite correctly) a rationalization. I couldn't confront the fact that I didn't have the self-assurance to walk out, so I blamed it on God—indirectly, through Father Louis.

Zirpoli was a fairly strict adherent to the Freudian tradition. I mean he was totally nondirective and nonreactive. For example, if I had told him (as I probably did) that my father thought I was a queer, he would simply have sat there, or he might have said, "Oh yes?" It was up to me to figure out where to go from there. He wasn't going to ask, for example, if I'd ever had any feelings of sexual attraction to a person of my own gender. I would've taken that as a sign that the presence or absence of such feelings had some bearing on the matter, and that wouldn't do.

The psychoanalyst isn't there to provide reassurance. He's there to provide a mirror in which you can see yourself. And at this point what I saw in the mirror had little relation to the image that was actually there. I was like an emaciated anorexic who looks in the mirror and sees someone who is fat, fat, fat, fat, fat.

What was wrong with me was not my sexual orientation. What was wrong with me was that I was so profoundly insecure that I needed someone else to tell me what my sexual orientation *was*. I had no *inner* assurance on the subject of my own identity. But of course I didn't see this at all. When I left his office after a session like this, I would be thinking: "Oh my God, maybe I *am* a queer."

After a year of this, I was living in a state of perpetual anxiety and inner tumult, which I imagine is par for the psychoanalytic course. When it comes to psychoanalysis, a year is just scratching the surface.

Meanwhile I fell in love, and this presented a crisis on several levels. In those days, for an earnest young man like me, to fall in love was to get married, and to get married would be to say good-bye to any possible return to the Trappist life. Perhaps even more distressing, to get married would be to adopt a lifestyle that, for a fundamentalist Roman Catholic, is spiritually second-rate. I assure you it's true. Heavens, read St. Paul! Marriage is something you do if you must, something you do if you can't manage without that filthy stuff called sex. Better to marry, Paul says, than to burn. Nowadays Catholics downplay this message, but it's there, loud and clear: Virgins occupy a distinctly higher spiritual plane than married folks. . . .

> *What was wrong with me was not my sexual orientation. What was wrong with me was that I was so profoundly insecure that I needed someone else to tell me what my sexual orientation was.*

Yes, this seems to contradict what I was saying a minute

ago, that I was no longer investing myself so totally in the cause of God. But in fact there's no contradiction here; if I'd still been investing myself totally in the cause of God, I wouldn't have allowed myself to fall in love at all. But once I'd fallen in love, I immediately began to question what I was doing. As I say, I simply didn't know what I was about, who I was, or what I wanted.

In addition to these reservations, there was this: Would I, as a married man, be able to pursue a career as a writer? I remember asking the poet Paul Carroll what he thought about this. He was clearly doubtful but wasn't comfortable giving me advice about such a thing. I asked a painter friend—himself married. He said, "If you don't marry Katherine, you'll always regret it." Believe it or not, I clung fervently to this advice. I gave this person's opinion far more weight than my own inclinations, because I wasn't sure I could trust them.

So one day I walked into Dr. Zirpoli's office and said, "Well, I'm going to get married!"

He was completely flabbergasted. He said, "I thought we agreed at the outset that you wouldn't make any major life decisions without reviewing them here."

It was my turn to be flabbergasted. It hadn't occurred to me that this was any of his concern. He suddenly ceased to be nondirective and told me in no uncertain terms that any marriage I entered into at this point would end in disaster. He couldn't have been more right, but I certainly didn't see any grounds for this dire prediction. In fact, I suspected him of simply wanting to keep me as a patient, which meant keeping me as my father's little boy.

However, since I'd created what he considered to be a

state of emergency, I agreed to start coming twice a week instead of once. I frankly don't remember what that accomplished, if anything. You can't make a crash course out of psychoanalysis. I'm sure he did his best and that he was moved by a genuine concern for me, but I was beyond help at that point. Not beyond it: simply not yet ready to receive it.

Someone whose self-esteem depends on being perfect is incapable of maintaining a relation of intimacy with anyone for very long. This is because, no matter how hard you try, you're going to slip up occasionally. In the beginning, before you've made any mistakes, you say to yourself, "Wow, Katherine thinks I'm wonderful, perfect, so naturally she loves me. That's why anybody loves anybody, because they think they're perfect." Then one time you slip up and you say to yourself, "Well, there goes a little bit of the gloss. Katherine now knows I'm only ninety-nine percent perfect; obviously her love has to be somewhat diminished, but I'll make it up to her by being twice as perfect, and she'll soon forget this small lapse." But this is just not a policy that's going to work for years and years. The gloss inevitably wears completely off of anybody, and this is disastrous for someone whose self-worth is bound up with being perfect.

> *Someone whose self-esteem depends on being perfect is incapable of maintaining a relation of intimacy with anyone for very long.*

After four years the matter was no longer in doubt:

Katherine *knew* I wasn't perfect. This wasn't important to *her*, mind you, this was important to *me*. My never-abundant self-confidence was completely gone, and everything else went with it. From the outset I'd been anything but a sexual athlete. I was still terrified of sex, still afraid to give myself over to sexual feelings, still worried that God must surely turn up his nose at such sweaty goings-on. Now, feeling completely worthless, far from being an athlete, I was a pathetic cripple, and this didn't work at all well for Katherine, who considered herself to be in the Olympic class. Somehow we struggled on, year after year, I vowing to improve, to become bigger and stronger, and instead growing weaker every day.

A battered wife will invest all her feelings of self-worth in her battering husband. She has totally accepted her husband's valuation of her, and this is why she stays: She hopes to redeem herself in her husband's eyes—and therefore in her own. I thought I loved Katherine desperately, but in fact my desperation was only to redeem myself in her eyes—and of course the more desperate I felt, the more pathetic I became.

When the youngest of our four children was well into toddlerhood, Katherine began to roam. She made no secret of this. She spent long evenings out "driving" and "thinking," and I absolutely believed that this was what she was doing, because I couldn't afford to believe anything else. One night I came home from a business trip, and she told me she wanted a divorce. I still didn't get it, and she finally had to draw me a picture. She didn't just want to get rid of me, she'd found herself another man—a *real* man—and they were going to get married as soon as she got her divorce and he got his. She had it all worked out. I could move into another bedroom until it was over or until the house was sold, whichever came first, then—

Fortunately, I found a sliver of a backbone in my body and said no thanks to that. My bag was there, all packed, so I just went and said good-bye to the kids and walked out.

Well, this was truly the end of the world for me, and for the first time in my life I didn't know where to turn. The universe was empty, the future as bleak as a prison sentence. I thought about suicide, and if I hadn't still believed in heaven and hell (and it's hell for suicides, of course), I might have done more than think about it.

I don't think there's any loneliness greater than the loneliness to be found in a bad marriage. In solitary confinement, everyone knows you're lonely and feels sorry for you. In a bad marriage loneliness is your darkest secret, one you dare not even share with your spouse. But now the secret was out. Everyone knew —and suddenly I had people to talk to for the first time in many years.

A young coworker by the name of Michael Carden lis-

> *I thought I loved Katherine desperately, but in fact my desperation was only to redeem myself in her eyes— and of course the more desperate I felt, the more pathetic I became.*

tened to my tale of woe . . . and chuckled. A bachelor and something of a lady-killer, this was someone whose experience and carnal wisdom were decades beyond my own. He assured me that it was not the end of the world for me, that in two months or six months I would feel nothing but relief to be out from under the burden of this terrible marriage, and he was quite right.

Again (and as always) you have to understand that I'm giving you the understanding of these events that I have now. My understanding of them at the time was quite different. What I'd told Michael Carden was that the failure of the marriage was due entirely to my sexual inadequacies, and this is what had made him chuckle. Katherine's expectations, Michael explained, were romantic nonsense, were the expectations of someone who hadn't been around much in the world as it is. Wild, passionate lovemaking among the long-married is a fantasy only Hollywood screenwriters believe in. She'd find this out after being married to her "real man" for a couple of years. In other words, according to Michael, Katherine's unrelenting assault on my feelings of self-worth was much more to blame for the failure of our marriage than my own shortcomings. Naturally I was delighted to adopt this interpretation of the affair.

Katherine and her new husband moved to St. Louis, taking the children, of course. Within a couple of years she was beginning to manifest some of the less attractive attributes of he-manhood, and she was speaking wistfully of her former husband's "thoughtfulness" and "sensitivity." The marriage struggled on for a few years, then ended in a noisy, rancorous divorce.

Thanks largely to sympathetic advisors like Michael, I began to come back to life. This was not an unmixed blessing, however, because the better I felt, the more painful my situation became. You see, according to the Church and my own belief, I was married to Katherine till death did us part, civil divorce notwithstanding. I was therefore condemned to a lifetime of chastity, and what was the good of having a new life if I could never share it with anyone in a relationship of real intimacy? Being a deadly serious Catholic, this was a deadly serious problem for me. Not a problem, really, because problems are things that have solutions, and this did not. I was just completely stuck.

Luckily, I talked about it to a coworker who was a Catholic, not looking for advice or ideas—I knew there weren't any—but simply bemoaning my fate. She suggested I talk to her brother, who was a priest. I couldn't imagine what good that would do, but I was desperate enough to try anything.

I believe he was a diocesan priest or a member of some order on loan to the diocese. I have a terrible memory for details like this. All I know is that he wasn't just an ordinary parish priest; for one thing, he'd had essays published in *Commonweal*, probably the country's leading journal of Roman Catholic thought. He was unusual in person as well; he lacked the patronizing attitude that laymen learn to expect from members of the clergy—he didn't try to pretend that there was no question on earth too tough for him to answer. We talked for awhile, and he listened to me explain the hopelessness of my situation. I think my plight made him uneasy—or rather, his reaction to my plight made him uneasy. He knew that if he told me what he truly thought, I'd be scandalized. (There's a word you don't hear much anymore.) Finally he spoke a few simple words that were to change the direction of my life once again. He said, "I find that the longer I live, the more I worry about *people* and the less I worry about *rules.*"

I doubt if you can imagine the impact these words had on me. This was practically a sacrilege, and of course doubly astounding coming from a priest. Not worry about *rules?* My God, if you don't worry about *rules* what *do* you worry about—if you're a Roman Catholic? The conversation was at an end. Nothing needed to be added to this bombshell. I staggered out of there in a state of shock.

The Church is a magnificent edifice, a structure composed of flawless, crystalline logic. It's like an enormous, perfect argument, unshakable and unassailable, and indeed inescapable—provided that you accept its premises. But its very perfection constitutes a weakness. You see, in a perfect argument there is no redundancy; every brick in the structure is necessary to the stability of the whole. This means that, if you pull a single brick out of that perfect structure, the whole thing collapses. This is why the Church has been so apparently stupid about refusing to moderate its stand on birth control. To someone on the inside, it's not at all stupid. The Church will only stand so long as every brick remains in place, and it's madness to think the pope himself is going to start pulling out bricks in order to placate the laity. The Church can go on perfectly well without the laity but will cease to exist if it compromises its own dogma. As far as the hierarchy is concerned, rewriting dogma to win popularity is cutting off your head to get rid of a headache: The ailment is temporary and endurable but the cure is permanent and lethal. . . .

No, that isn't quite what I mean. It isn't just that the Church "stands for something." It's more than that.

This is worth spending a little time on. In *Ishmael* I articulated a living mythology that is so integral to our culture that it's never examined or even noticed by anyone. It's like the sound of blood rushing through your veins—you hear it so constantly that you don't hear it at all. A similarly unarticulated mythology has driven the Church from the beginning. The Church's mythological vision of itself and of its function in the world was so well-known and so unquestionably accepted (through the first fifteen hundred years of its existence) that it didn't need to be articulated—didn't need to be explained or pointed out to anyone.

> *Finally he spoke a few simple words that were once again to change the direction of my life. He said, "I find that the longer I live, the more I worry about* **people** *and the less I worry about* **rules.**"

Here is how it came to be understood: God has made two covenants with man during man's lifetime. The first he made with the Jews, and the results were decidedly unsatisfactory. As a Chosen People, the Jews were a wash-out. They flouted the laws he gave them, they much pre-ferred to worship their neighbors' gods, they scorned the prophets he sent them, and generally ignored the whole thing. Nevertheless, though they didn't keep up their end of the bargain, God kept up his: He sent them the mes-siah he'd promised, and the only thing they could think to do with him was to have him put to death. (Once again, you understand that I'm not expressing my own views here but rather the Church's.)

The New Covenant was designed to avoid the errors of the Old. The Old Covenant was based on the notion that God could deal with a few selected individuals who would transmit his directives to the Jews at large, and the Jews in turn would pass these directives on to their children. It made perfect sense in theory but didn't work out well in practice. Let me give you an example. The event God wanted the Hebrews to remember most conscientiously was their liberation from Egypt, which occurred in about 1210 B.C. This event, which was to be commemorated as Passover, exemplified in a definitive way the kind of care and attention they could expect from God if they would be faithful to him. But once they were finally allowed to enter the Holy Land after forty years of wandering in the desert, the first thing they did was abandon the celebra-tion of Passover. Not a single Passover was held under all the judges and kings of Israel until the eighteenth year of the reign of Josiah, just a few years before the Babylonian exile began. During all that time—six hundred years!—the Israelites worshiped not the God who had led them from Egypt but rather the gods and goddesses of the

Sidonians and the Amorites and the Moabites and the Philistines and the Babylonians. During most of this time, if you'd asked them about the God of Israel, they wouldn't even have known what God you were talking about. This is literally true. Their gods were Baal and Ashtaroth and Dagon and Azazel and Milcom and Asima and Succoth Benoth and Anamelech and Nergal and Kemosh and Moloch. And if you'd asked them to point out a priest, it would have been one who burnt offerings to Baal or who tended one of the hill shrines. . . .

Oh, yes, the temple was set up in Jerusalem. No doubt about that. And inside that temple you'd have found altars dedicated to all those gods and goddesses—except for Moloch; he was set up in the valley of the sons of Hinnom. And attached to the temple you'd have found quarters for the temple prostitutes—male prostitutes.

The New Covenant was designed to avoid the errors of the Old, which had proved to be a flop.

The Mosaic teachings had been abandoned from the outset—abandoned and then lost. It was Josiah who rediscovered them around 610 B.C., and Judaism as we know it began with this event—not with Abraham, not with the Exodus, not with the Israelites' entry into the land of Canaan.

So you can see why I say that this system had proved to be a flop. There'd been a monumental lapse in continuity, and the New Covenant would be structured so as to assure continuity. Under the New Covenant, religion would no longer be a family affair or an ethnic affair, it would be a corporate affair, an institutional affair. There was going to be something wholly new in the history of the world, something never even heard of before: a *church*. Jesus said to Simon, son of Jonah, "I'm going to give you a new name. I'm going to call you *rock—peter—* and on this rock I'm going to build a strange new thing called a church." Then he added this: "And the power of death shall never conquer it." This was very significant, of course. The Old Covenant had depended for its continuity on *individuals,* and this is how the power of death conquered it. Abraham died, Moses died, David died, Isaiah died, Jeremiah died—and God's contact with the Jews through them was therefore ineffectual. Under the New Covenant, death would no longer have the power to interrupt the continuity of God's contact with mankind. This thing called a church would not be built on prophets or families or peoples. It would be built on a rock, on a foundation that would *hold things together*. Here is how it would hold things together: To Peter Jesus next said, "I'm going to give you the keys to the kingdom of heaven itself. What you forbid on earth will be forbidden in heaven and what you permit on earth will be permitted in heaven." Obviously the keys weren't meant to be buried with Peter when he died; there'd be no continuity in that. The keys were meant to be passed along to Peter's successor, who would pass them along to his. Otherwise there'd be no rock, and the church would pass away after a single generation.

This can't be stressed too strongly: The rock on which Jesus founded his church was not a *text,* it was a *deputy,* a stand-in for Christ himself, who would speak for Christ

and wield a power that had never existed on earth before.
It was a whole new concept, a whole new dispensation. In
the old dispensation, God would pick out someone and
say, "Tell everyone that this is what is permitted and this
is what is forbidden." Never again would it be done this
way. In the new dispensation, his permanently established
deputy—one of *us*, a human living right in our midst—
was going to decide what's permitted and what's forbidden, and we had the word of Christ that his deputy's
decisions would be ratified in heaven!

The New Covenant put mankind and God in an entirely new relation. In the old dispensation, God tried to
do everything himself, and his chosen people weren't expected to participate in a very
active way—and they didn't.
Under the Old Covenant,
people were clearly put too
much on their own, given too
much leeway. The church of
the new dispensation was going to change all that. This was
going to be an *organization*.
People weren't going to be
put on their own, they were
going to be watched over and
guarded like a flock of sheep.
And they were going to be given extraordinary new
means of participation in their own salvation. Entirely
new institutions called *sacraments* opened channels to divine grace that had never been available before. The human race and God—earth and heaven—were to be joined

> *Under the Old
> Covenant, people
> were put too much
> on their own, given
> too much leeway.
> The church of the
> new dispensation
> was going to change
> all that.*

in a new mystical intimacy: Holy Mother Church was the bride of Christ, forever yearning to be united with him.

The Church (and now we begin again to speak of the Church with a capital C) didn't see itself as merely the trustee and conservator of a revelation that had occurred and ended in the past. The conversation between Christ and his bride would continue to the end of time, and this is why no great emphasis was ever placed on reading the bible. Your source of revealed truth wasn't an ancient text to which not a single word could ever be added, it was the living Church. If you wanted to know what was what, you didn't reach for your bible, you asked your priest, and if your priest didn't know, he'd ask the bishop, and if the bishop didn't know, he'd ask the cardinal, and if the cardinal didn't know, he'd ask the pope. The Vicar of Christ, speaking *ex cathedra*—from the chair of St. Peter—spoke with precisely the same authority as the apostle, and what he bound on earth was bound in heaven and what he loosed on earth was loosed in heaven.

Within its own ranks, the Protestant Reformation cleared away all this rich mythology to make room for a much simplified and more austere vision of the relation between God and man. With the bible now available to virtually everyone, thanks to the advancement of printing technology, it seemed self-evident to the Protestant mind that nothing like the Church and certainly nothing like the pope needed to stand between the individual and his or her God. As it was now understood, the keys to the kingdom were in Everyman's hand.

I say "within its own ranks," referring to the Protestant Reformation. The Church itself never relinquished its

own vision and will never do so unless it loses its mind—
becomes confused about its own identity. Until that happens, ecumenical negotiators will never see the primacy of
Peter become a chip on the bargaining table. That is indeed the rock upon which the Church is built, and any
ecumenical movement that hopes to include the Church
will inevitably be shattered on it. . . .

Yes, you're quite right, I would have made a powerful
apologist for the Church. Perhaps only an apostate can
fully appreciate its glamour and magnificence—glamour
in its original sense of "enchantment" and "magic."

What the priest had done with
his casual remark about rules
was to show me that the rock
of papal primacy was standing
in a desert. According to Peter
and his successors, divorce and
remarriage were forbidden, no
two ways about it. What the
priest had said was: Yes, you're
right, this is certainly the rule,
but . . . maybe rules don't matter all that much.

> *The priest's remark
> about rules had
> shown me that the
> rock of papal
> primacy was
> standing in a desert.*

Now this priest was obviously not speaking *ex cathedra*.
The Church wasn't revising its estimate of the importance
of rules—hardly. According to the fundamental notions
of the Church, forbidding and permitting is what it's all
about, and Jesus himself made this crystal clear in his di-
rective to Peter. And it isn't just a little part. If you look at
that passage in Matthew, you'll see it's the whole job de-

scription. Now I had to compare this priest with the God who had conceived of this new dispensation. It took about ten seconds to see that I liked and admired this priest a whole hell of a lot better than I liked and admired this God. What kind of God is it who worries more about rules than about people? I didn't doubt that this God existed, I simply doubted that he deserved my allegiance. Was he seriously proposing to send me to hell for eternity if I remarried? If yes, he was a monster. If no, he was a liar. Either way, as I saw it then and today, he deserves nothing but my contempt. . . .

Yes, this is a question that has been posed in various ways by many people. Why didn't I turn to some denomination in which divorce and remarriage is countenanced? This misses the point. My quarrel was not with the rules but with God. Do the Episcopalians worship a different God from the Catholics? Do the Lutherans worship a different God from the Catholics? There's no doubt about the answer to that one. No one would disagree: They all worship the same God. What separates and distinguishes these sects is not the God they worship but their take on what he permits and what he forbids. The issue is always rules, whether it's strict rules, lenient rules, or even no rules at all. If you're gay, you can join this denomination because, according to them, being gay is permitted. If you believe women have a right to abort an unwanted child, you'd better not join this denomination, because, according to them, abortion is definitely forbidden except in rare cases.

No, I hadn't the slightest interest in shopping around for a denomination with rules that suited the way I wanted to live. I turned my back on that God entirely and have never missed him for a single moment. . . .

I understand the urgency of that question, and we'll definitely get to it eventually. All I can say right now is that I didn't say, "There is no God." What I said was, "If there is a God and he's the way the Christians say he is, then I renounce him. I despise him and will have nothing to do with him."

And of course there remained that hour at Gethsemani. Turning my back on the God of the Christians gave me no insight into that at all. Why would it?

NINE

By the time I was three years out of college, I
was the head of the biography and fine arts department of
APE—the American Peoples Encyclopedia. My dream of
becoming a fiction writer began to lose some of its allure
as I saw a career in publishing open up before me. I was
working with two astonishingly competent and knowl-
edgeable people: Francis Squibb, who had been the biography and fine arts editor before me and was now the
managing editor, and Ruth Hunt, who had been the
managing editor before Francis and was now the editor-
in-chief. From these two I'd learned more about writing
in six months than in all my years in school.

I had the absurd idea that the pattern of my life was set;

in another five or ten years, we'd all move up another step
—Ruth to a vice presidency, Francis to editor-in-chief,
and I to managing editor—and five or ten years after that
I'd be the editor-in-chief myself. I was innocent of the
ways of the publishing world. In less than two years, the
encyclopedia had been sold to Grolier and moved to New
York, Ruth had been let go, Francis had been invited to
come along to New York in an indefinite capacity, and I'd
declined a similar invitation. I couldn't have imagined it
then, but in the nearly twenty-five years that followed I
would never again work in an environment where admin-
istrative competence was the rule rather than the exception, where supervisors could be relied on to know more
than their subordinates, where ability counted for more
than having a good front or standing in well with the
right people.

Ruth Hunt had taken a job in the math department at
Science Research Associates and invited me to join her
there. I accepted, though moving into educational publishing struck me as a lackluster and disappointing career
step. As had happened so many times before and was to
happen so many times afterward, however, the step that
seemed to lead away from my life's work ultimately
proved to be a direct step toward it.

If ever there was a golden age in educational publishing,
the early sixties was it. Federal funds were pouring into
the schools, and, since the rule is "Use it or lose it," the
schools were spending prodigiously. Fortunes were being
made by materials producers, and by the mid-sixties, all

the high-tech giants like Xerox and IBM would be looking for educational subsidiaries.

The age was golden for other reasons. The fact that the Soviets had beaten us into space with Sputnik put a world-size spotlight on the backwardness of our school programs, particularly in math and science. Sweeping changes were needed, and innovation was the rallying cry. Incredible new media and technologies were going to revolutionize the classroom. B. F. Skinner was hot stuff, and programmed instruction was practically going to make teachers obsolete.

As was to happen so many times, the step that seemed to lead away from my life's work ultimately proved to be a direct step toward it.

The old-line, big-name publishers of the past were not really comfortable with all this, though they had to sound as though they were. They were used to developing highly traditional materials at a stately and gentlemanly pace. By contrast, revolutionary times were perfect for Lyle Spencer, the founder of SRA. He was an innovator by instinct, and he didn't see any virtue in dawdling. In a period of a few years, he had moved from being a small specialty publisher to being the industry leader that everyone had to struggle to keep up with.

I wasn't aware of any of this at the time, so I didn't realize how lucky I was to be there. Ruth and I were rather like the mandarins of Broadway who went out to Hollywood in the early days of filmmaking; it all seemed a bit crude and slipshod to us, and it was. The received wisdom of the industry was (and is) that you hire teachers to design and write your materials, which is rather like hiring musicians to design and build your opera house. Some have a talent for it, but most don't, and why should they? The skills you need to put ideas across in a classroom are entirely different from the skills you need to put ideas across in a book or a motion picture or a set of visuals and tapes.

May I ask when you started school? Yes, that's what I figured. You came too late to have a taste of what was then called Modern Mathematics. That's what I was working on at SRA: the Greater Cleveland Mathematics Program, one of the first, best, and most ambitious New Math projects of the sixties. The whole New Math movement was intended to flush down the drain the old-fashioned rote-learned mathematics that I'd grown up with. The idea was that the old math was okay for farmers and salesclerks, but if you wanted to produce mathematicians and scientists, you had to teach math in a way that made *sense* to the kids who were learning it. As far as I was concerned, this was a terrific idea. Kids brought up on the New Math were obviously going to be vastly better prepared for the modern world than the kids of my generation, who were mostly mathematically illiterate—and rather smug about it as well.

It turned out, however, that there was a fundamental flaw in this idea. As expected, a lot of kids really thrived on the New Math (as I would have done, as a child), but an equally large number of kids were just being left in the dark by it. They were neither making sense out of it nor learning it by rote (since it wasn't being *taught* by rote), so they basically weren't learning anything at all. So the New Math ultimately went on the trash heap of discarded ideas.

What people failed to consider was that, just as there are two fundamentally different ways to teach math, there are two fundamentally different kinds of kids trying to learn it. But no, you can't have two different ways, our educational system won't accommodate that; it has to be one way or the other. This was my introduction to one of the fundamental concepts that drive our culture: the concept of the One Right Way. There can't be *good* ways of teaching something, there has to be a *right* way—one and only way, with all other ways *wrong*.

> *This was my introduction to a fundamental concept of our culture: the concept of the One Right Way.*

I hadn't till then given much thought to the way we educate our kids. Who does? For someone bent on achievement, education is a thing you get past and forget about as quickly as possible. This is particularly true of elementary and secondary education, of course. These are only important to the extent that they contribute to putting you in a good college or university. Now that I began to look at it critically, however, I began to remember what it had been like: the tremendous excitement of the first couple of years, when kids imagine that great secrets are going to be unfolding before them, then the disappointment that gradually sets in when you begin to realize the truth: There's plenty of learning to do, but it's not the learning you wanted. It's learning to keep your mouth shut, learning how to avoid attracting the teacher's attention when you don't want it, learning not to ask questions, learning how to pretend to understand, learning how to tell teachers what they want to hear, learning to keep your own ideas and opinions to yourself, learning how to look as if you're paying attention, learning how to endure the endless boredom.

The child isn't capable of asking, "Why is it like this?" School is the way it is, the way parents are the way they are. This is the universe. This is the given.

Now, approaching age thirty, I *was* capable of asking it. It has always been my special gift (and my special curse) to ask the questions no one else seems to need an answer to.

After five years in educational publishing I found myself dedicated to the task of overthrowing a school system that seemed to me inhuman and unproductive. Religion wasn't the future, science wasn't the future. Education was the future. Education was salvation for mankind— which is to say for *us,* the people of my culture; I was a decade away from realizing that it's a cultural solecism to speak of the future of mankind as *our* future. What I was thinking at that time was, if we could break free of the tyranny of the schools, we had a chance of finding that paradise we'd all been trying to fashion for ourselves here for thousands of years.

As you can see, I was beginning to grope my way toward a vein of radical ideas uniquely my own, and the field of educational publishing, which I had at first taken for a side track, now began to look like it might be the main track after all.

TEN

Forgive me. I haven't been asleep, I've been groping for a direction, and it appears to be this. The next decade, roughly 1965 to 1975, served only one real purpose in my life: It deranged my habitual expectations.

I grew up a charter member of the Silent Generation. You've probably never heard of it. I think the name was coined in an article in the *Atlantic* in about 1955, but, characteristically, there was no rebuttal from us, so the name didn't catch on in any big way.

We were the first generation to grow up in the shadow of the mushroom cloud, the first generation to grow up with the knowledge that all of this could be gone in an hour—and probably *would* be gone, one of these days. It may be hard for you to imagine, with the Cold War receding into the distant past, but nuclear holocaust was on people's minds then the way AIDS is now. It was right there. One day you'd be looking out the window, and there it would be. People like Malenkov and Bulganin and Khrushchev were practically lunatics, who might well be willing to destroy the entire world for the satisfaction of destroying us. And we had lunatics of our own who would have been happy to push the button. Unless you lived through the Cuban Missile Crisis, you can't have any idea of what it was like.

We of the Silent Generation were like children tiptoeing through a roomful of sleeping mad dogs. This is almost literally true. We kept our mouths shut and hoped for the best, and the best we could think of was a few years in which to collect some modest toys of our own. We wanted a nice, safe career, a nice, safe family, a nice, safe house in the suburbs, a pair of television sets, a pair of cars in the garage, and a well-stocked bomb shelter in the backyard. We weren't looking for adventure or for fun or for self-realization, we were looking for *security*.

I was no exception. The first thing I did on leaving college was to get married. That was essential. And within five years, by God, we had that house in the suburbs. Given a few more years, we would've had the rest as well. By then we were miserable, of course, but I could have endured years more of that, for the sake of a quiet, safe life, all planned out and getting a tiny bit better every single year. But not Katherine. She opened her mouth and shattered the silence. As much as anything else, it was the need to resume the fantasy of a quiet, safe life that drove me toward remarriage within a couple of years.

The appearance of the Flower Children in the mid-sixties bowled me over. Not because they were dirty, not because they preferred dressing in rags, not because they let their hair grow, but because they'd stopped thinking about the bomb. I hadn't dreamed it was possible to do that. For us, the bomb was new and everlastingly urgent. For them, it was old and boring. For us, the answer was a house in the suburbs and a secure future. For them, the answer was fun and dope and music and sex and love. For them, the answer was to live now instead of waiting till your pension kicked in.

The appearance of the Flower Children in the mid-sixties bowled me over.

They said, "You can't trust anyone over thirty," and I said, "Hold on, I may be over thirty—by a hair!—but you can trust *me*." I knew they were onto something, you see. My generation's desperate clutching onto what is safe and solid and material was a sickness. The Flower Children were right to reject the values and goals we'd grown up with. I saw all this, so I took exception to their rule about being over thirty. I was a few years away from seeing it, but they were right and I was wrong—even in my own case.

The sexual revolution doomed my second marriage, which might well have dragged on for years otherwise. It was failing for much the same reasons as the first. My shallow self-esteem couldn't survive my failure to achieve perfection. Mary wasn't prepared to demand as much from life as Katherine, so she was willing to put up with this. The trouble was, I wasn't. I was now no longer ready to settle down to a placid, secure life. I wanted much, much more. Suddenly I wanted adventure, I wanted romance—I wanted in on that revolution! Although I'd lived as a bachelor for a couple of years between marriages, I really hadn't done much living. Now I meant to cut loose, now I meant to sow wild oats by the truckload!

Well, I was a pathetic creature. I had no more idea what life in the real world was all about than a three-year-old does. I'd listened to the lessons of my old tutor, Michael Carden, and hadn't understood a word of them.

Have you ever seen Arte Johnson's Dirty Old Man on *Laugh-In*? It's a brilliant characterization. But the odd thing is, his Dirty Old Man isn't really a dirty old man at all, because he's totally honest about his intentions, totally honest with himself and totally honest with the women he encounters. At age thirty-five, *I* was a dirty old man, because I was a liar. I lied to myself and I lied to every woman I met—not intentionally or consciously, mind you. It was simply my impression that there was no way to establish a relationship with any woman except through deception. It was my estimate that any woman would reject me if I allowed her to see me as I really was.

I wanted women to believe I was a liberated man (and I thought I was), when in fact I was merely a would-be libertine, which liberated women picked up on in about three seconds. I thought there was just some little trick I needed to learn; I thought maybe my technique needed a little work. I deceived myself in these ways for as long as I could manage it, a year or so, then I gradually began to be persuaded that there was a much deeper point that I was missing, and that I needed some help in finding it. After fifteen years and two failed marriages, I was finally ready for psychotherapy.

I was tremendously lucky to find a wonderful therapist, Dr. Ada Saichy, a Jew who managed to get out of Europe just ahead of the Final Solution. Although she'd practiced for years in Czechoslovakia, her home, she'd had to go back to school for a new doctoral degree here (though of course that was long ago). Her orientation, like Dr. Zirpoli's, was fundamentally Freudian, but her method was eclectic rather than strictly psychoanalytic.

Everything I told you about my childhood was shaped by what I learned during the two years I worked with Madame Saichy. I certainly didn't come to her with the understanding that I had a compulsive need

After fifteen years and two failed marriages, I was finally ready for psychotherapy.

to be perfect, based on the mistaken notion that being perfect would make me lovable. These were things we worked out during the course of long months of effort. I gradually came to understand that perfection was my substitute for adequacy: If I was perfect, no one would notice how worthless I was.

And how did I come to think of myself as worthless? That was easily answered, though the answer seemed to do me no good. My parents had convinced me I was worthless—in a thousand ways that I won't bore you with

—but knowing this fact didn't help, because as far as I could see they were absolutely right. Stripped of my perfection, what was I good for? Not a damned thing, as far as I could see. Oh, I was a hell of a writer and editor, and a pretty good boss, but who cares about things like that? As a *person*, I was a washout. My entire strategy with people I met (especially women, of course) was to trick them into thinking I was someone worth knowing— someone perhaps even worth loving. Every word, every gesture, had to be calculated to this end. Everything I did was a lie, because the truth was that I was utterly hollow. This was what had to be hidden, my devastating secret. In this undertaking, spontaneity was obviously the greatest enemy. To be spontaneous would be to reveal the great yawning emptiness inside of me.

When I reached this point of understanding, after perhaps a year, Madame Saichy said to me, "You know, there really isn't very much wrong with you," and I laughed, having at last figured out just how *much* was wrong with me. But she persisted. "There will come a day," she said, "when you'll be flooded with self-esteem. It won't happen in an hour or a day or a week, but the time will come when you'll be able to look at yourself and recognize your own worth without a shadow of a doubt."

I shook my head, knowing that this hopeless prediction was meant to encourage me but unable to give it the least credit. She might as well have said that I would one day find a magic lantern with three wishes in it. She knew of course that I was incapable of taking her word for this— or of even understanding what she was talking about.

Nevertheless, as things turned out, it happened just the way she predicted, except for one detail: It *did* happen in an hour.

I suppose it must have been half a year later. I was profoundly stuck and profoundly discouraged. Nothing had happened in months. I understood how I'd gotten this way, but so what? My parents' estimate of me was that I was about as wonderful as a wart, and all I could see was that they were right. I said to Madame Saichy, "For God's sake, if you see something of value in me, tell me what it is!"

"That I cannot do—must not do," she replied (of course). "What *I* see doesn't matter. Only what *you* see matters. It is *you* who must esteem yourself, not me. Without self-esteem, the esteem of others is worthless."

I left her office at an all-time low. In fact, I was so desperate that I was willing to try something completely silly. Bussing down Sheridan Road on my way to work, I took out a scrap of paper, a bank deposit receipt or something, and headed it with these words: *Things that are good about me.* I was sure that, having taken this brave but foolhardy step, I wasn't going to be able to think of a single thing to write, but, by golly, suddenly words were pouring out of my pen: *I'm reasonably trustworthy, I can keep a secret, I'm never deliberately cruel, I honor my promises, I'm fair, I can see things from other people's point of view, I can own up to my mistakes,* and so on. I can't remember all I wrote. A lot of it was nonsense anyway, but that didn't matter. The clouds parted and rushed off toward the horizon the way they do in stop-motion photography. The light flooded in, and it all came clear. I was transformed—not in an hour, in a single minute. It was literally all over. Just as Madame Saichy had said, I was flooded with self-esteem, and it was never going to go away.

It wasn't that I'd found a collection of virtues that made me lovable. In the course of writing out my list, I'd stumbled on the key insight: What makes people lovable isn't being perfect, it's simply being *human* and, reading that list, I saw that that's what I was. I was *within the range.* Just as Madame Saichy had said, *there wasn't much wrong with me.* I wasn't a saint (which is what I'd hoped to be when I was trying to be perfect), but I also wasn't a monster (which is how I'd come to view myself in the past two years). I was *human.* I was *ordinary.* I was like *other* people, and if other people are worthy of love, then so was I! Why on earth *shouldn't* people love me?

And I suddenly saw that, just as I was like other people, other people were like *me.* Even *women* were like me, because they too were human. I was waiting for them to love me—and, being just like me, they were also waiting for me to love them. They *wanted* my love! And why the hell not?

By the time I reached my office, I was literally a changed man. I was a foot taller. I was ready to embrace everyone in my path. At last I understood the obvious truth. No one wanted me to be perfect. Everyone wanted me to be like them—and I was. I was *one of them.* At the age of thirty-seven, I had at last joined the human race. I no longer had to guard against spontaneity. People *wanted* me to be spontaneous. Nobody cared if I made mistakes. Nobody was watching to *see* if I made mistakes. I was free of all that.

The needy are insatiable. I know that because I was once one of them. I was like hundreds of millions of men in our culture. The hollowness inside of me was so vast that the love of one woman was not nearly enough to fill it. Who's the basketball player who boasts of having had ten thousand women? Men typically regard this as a tremendous, enviable success. They wish *they* could have ten thousand women—a million women! This isn't a measure of their virility (as they like to imagine); it's a measure of their incalculable neediness.

Now, for the first time in my life, I had left the ranks of the needy. I was no longer insatiable. I no longer needed every woman in the world. One would be enough. I no longer had to make a try for every single woman who crossed my path. This meant that genuine friendship with women was possible.

I suddenly saw that, just as I was like other people, they were like me. Even women were like me, because they too were human.

From that point on, I no longer had to *pretend* to be liberated. From the moment we met, women knew I was following no hidden agenda with regard to them.

They knew I wasn't just feeding them a line, wasn't scheming for a way to get something from them they weren't prepared to give.

This book that I'm talking here tonight with you—you didn't know it was a book, but it is—this book, I've decided, will be called *Providence*. . . .

How do I define *Providence*? I'll answer that the way a mathematician will answer you if you ask for a definition of the word *set*. In mathematics *set* is an undefined term. Unless you're a mathematician (or are used to dealing with mathematicians), you will demand to know how on earth you can have a study or a theory that is based on an undefined term, but this will get you nowhere. In this book *Providence* is an undefined term. This is a book *about* Providence, a book in which one can *learn* about Providence, without ever having it defined. Every time you hear me say, "It was my good fortune at this point that . . ." or "As luck would have it . . ." or "If this thing had happened just one week earlier . . ." or words to that effect, you'll know I'm talking about Providence. I may have given you the impression that this book is about me or about the origins of *Ishmael,* but in fact it's about Providence . . . whatever that may be.

Now . . .

A week after this great transformative epiphany was the occasion of our annual Christmas party at Fuller & Dees Publishing, where I was the executive editor, second in command. This wasn't your ordinary Christmas party, an office party with Christmas decorations. Our way of doing business was to have a small core staff and an army of freelancers: writers, designers, editors, illustrators, and so on, and this party was for all of them, along with another small army of printing salesmen, paper salesmen, typesetters, and so on. This was quite a bash.

One of the women at the party was a freelance writer who was working on a project of mine. I have the impression that I'd talked to her for an hour total in the course of our business. She evidently liked to keep this sort of contact at a minimum, because when an assignment was due, I'd find it shoved under the door when I arrived in the morning. I had my eye on her this night. I watched with great amusement as one of the printing salesmen started putting the moves on her. Having been there myself, I knew exactly what was going through his mind. I actually saw him slip his wedding ring off and pocket it. When he picked up the telephone, I moved close enough to hear him call his wife and explain that he might be a little later than he thought.

I watched him romancing her with glum calculation, waiting for his moment, waiting, waiting, waiting till the time would be just right for him to say, "Hey, would you like to have dinner with me?"

It was expected of me that I'd stick around at least until the party peaked and began to run downhill. When it finally did, I went over to where this writer and printing salesman were standing and said to her, "Hi. Would you like to go get a hamburger?"

Both of them looked a little stunned, but she quickly said, "Sure," and went to get her coat.

The printing salesman's eyes were bugging out as he goggled at me in bafflement. Finally he said—believe it or not—"Can I come too?"

I said, with elegant simplicity: "No."

And that was that. That was how it began between Rennie and me.

One week after making the discovery that I didn't need all the women in the world, I only needed one, I found the only one I needed. A week earlier I wouldn't have been ready for her, I would have been no better off than that dumb printing salesman. A week earlier I would have been incapable of simply walking up and issuing an invitation. A week earlier I wouldn't have dreamed of inviting her to anything but the most extravagant restaurant in Chicago. A week earlier I wouldn't have had nearly enough self-confidence to tell the printing salesman to get lost.

One week. One week makes it Providence.

That I was ready for Rennie was providential not only for me but for her. Ours was a great love story—but a story for another time. Dawn is soon going to be making itself felt out there.

Removing the dominating handicap of my emotional life didn't free me of problems. Rather, it freed me to recognize that I had a different sort of problem to solve, which was to find a direction for my life.

You need two points to determine a line. Fixed only at

its pivot point, the needle of a compass can do nothing but spin round and round uselessly; it must have a second point to fix its direction: magnetic north. The point I was spinning round and round was that hour at Gethsemani. That was my pivot point. I didn't see that I had another point, which was that mysterious and compelling dream I'd had at age six. But even if I'd been able to guess that these two points determined a line, I would not have been able to see what the line was pointing to.

I was wandering around in the middle of my life without a compass. I needed someone to show me the way. I needed a guide, a teacher—and this is what I told Madame Saichy, whom I was still seeing even though I was clearly no longer in need of psychotherapy. This was the first she'd heard of this, and she asked me what I needed a teacher for. I don't remember how I explained it. The model I had in mind was rather like a spiritual director. I wanted someone who would assume a genuine *responsibility* for my future, the way Father Louis had. I wanted someone with superhuman insight who would be able to look at the compass of my life and know how to stop the needle from its endless, meaningless spinning. Who would be able to say, "Here. Here is

Without having the least idea what I was doing, I set out to become my own teacher.

the second point that fixes the line. Here is your direction. This is what Providence has been shaping your life toward."

Well, Madame Saichy listened patiently, and when I was

finished she said, "You don't need a teacher. You will be your *own* teacher."

I'm sure I must have laughed at this notion. I explained that to talk about being your own teacher is like talking about being your own parent. To try to be your own teacher is like trying to pull yourself up by your boot-straps. No matter. When I finished rolling out all my objections, she said again, "You will be your own teacher."

Madame Saichy made only two predictions in the time that I knew her, and, though I scoffed at both, both came true.

In another five years or so, without having the least idea that that was what I was doing, I would set out to become my own teacher.

Before this could come about, however, it was necessary to put paid to my illusions about using educational publishing as an instrument of change in the world. (I think I can safely begin to speak more openly in this vein.)

One of the great, persistent myths of education in our culture is that children become reluctant learners as they grow older. In fact, what they become reluctant about is going to school, where they're bullied, regimented, bored silly, and very effectively prevented from learning. The learning curve of small children is simply phenomenal during the first five years of their life. They learn the language of their parents—several languages, if several are spoken. They learn four fifths of the vocabulary they'll use in their everyday activities for the rest of their lives. They easily learn to walk, run, skip, swim, ride a bicycle, draw, print, count, and hundreds of other things they'll do for the rest of their lives (including reading, if parents will give them a little help). But as soon as they enter school, this learning curve begins to level off, and within a few years it's practically flat. And the *children* are blamed for this. In effect, the educators say, "See? If it weren't for the hard work we do, these kids wouldn't be learning ANYTHING!"

One of the absolute principles of education that every teacher learns is that children learn something very easily when they're *ready* to learn it, which is to say, when they *want* to learn it. The classic example is batting averages. Kids who become interested in baseball learn to figure batting averages without the slightest effort—without being "taught" at all. It's as though they take it in through their pores. Children find this operation *extremely* difficult to learn when it's taught as a subject in class, but if they have a *reason* to learn it—their *own* reason—they learn it in no time.

As I say, everyone in education knows this—but they would never dream of allowing children to learn this way as a general rule. That wouldn't do at all, because of course how would you *organize* such a thing? How can you possibly know when a given child will develop a *reason* to learn how to read a map? And what would you do when you found out? No, the only way to *organize* learning is to give chil-

> *As soon as children enter school, their learning curve begins to level off, and the children are blamed for this.*

dren a reason to learn *all at the same time*. This is called *motivating* them. You have thirty children in your class and the curriculum says it's time to teach them some map-reading skills, so now you *motivate* them to learn about maps. You try to manufacture something that approximates the interest kids have when they learn to figure batting averages.

Of course it doesn't work, that goes without saying. No one *expects* it to work. When kids learn to figure batting averages, they're responding to a motivation that arises within *them*. This is something *they* want to do. Map reading is something *you* want them to do. No matter. Your task is to "motivate," so you "motivate"—the more the better.

Our entire program is based on this argument: "We know kids learn effortlessly if they have their *own* reasons for learning, but we can't wait for them to find their own reasons. We have to provide them with reasons that are *not* their own. This doesn't work and we *know* it doesn't work, but it's the only *practical* way to organize our schools."

What? How would *I* organize the schools? To ask this question presupposes that we *must* have schools, doesn't it? I prefer to think about problems the way engineers do. If a valve doesn't work, they don't say, "Well, we *must* have valves, so let's try *two* valves." If a valve doesn't work, they say, "Well, what *would* work?" Their rule is, if it doesn't work, don't do it *more*, do *something else*.

We know what works for children up to the age where

we ship them off to school: Let them be around you, pay attention to them, talk to them, give them access to as much as you can, let them try things, and that's it. They'll take care of the rest. You don't have to strap small children down and *teach* them to speak, all you have to do is talk to them. You don't have to give them crawling lessons or walking lessons or running lessons. You don't have to spend an hour a day showing them how to bang two pots together; they'll figure that out all by themselves —if you give them access to the pots.

Nothing magical happens at the age of five to render this process obsolete or invalid. You would know this if you observed what happens in cultures that we in our arrogant stupidity call *primitive*. In primitive cultures, parents simply go on keeping the children around, paying attention to them, talking to them, giving them access to everything, letting them try out things for themselves, and that's it. They don't herd them together for courses in tracking, pottery making, plant cultivation, hunting, and so on. That's totally unnecessary. They don't give them history lessons or craft lessons or art lessons or music lessons,

> *We know what works: Give them access to as much as you can. Nothing magical happens at the age of five to render this process obsolete.*

but—magically—all the kids grow up knowing their history, knowing their crafts, knowing their arts, knowing their music. Every kid grows up knowing *everything*— without a single minute spent in anything remotely like a school. No tests, no grades, no report cards. Every kid learns everything there is to learn in that culture because sooner or later every kid feels within himself or herself the *need* to learn it—just the way some kids in our culture get to a point where they feel the need to learn how to compute batting averages. . . .

Yes, I understand—believe me, I do. What you're saying is exactly what our educators would say: "That system might work in primitive cultures, but it won't work in ours, because we just have *too much to learn.*" This is just ethnocentric balderdash; you might not like to hear this, but any anthropologist will confirm it: What children learn in other cultures isn't *less,* it's *different.* And in fact nothing is too much to learn if kids want to learn it. Take the case of teenage computer hackers. These kids, because they want to, manage—unaided!—to achieve a degree of computer sophistication that matches or surpasses that of whole teams of people with advanced degrees and decades of experience. Give kids access and they'll learn. Restrict their access to what you think they should learn, and they won't—and this is the function of our schools, to restrict kids' access to learning, to give them what educators think they should know, when they think they should know it, one drop at a time.

Are you able to remember yourself at age five, seven, nine, ten? Do you recall yearning to be allowed to sit in a classroom for six hours a day? No, neither do I. Do you remember where you wanted to be? Or can you imagine where you *might* have wanted to be? Well, yes, certainly out-of-doors, not in a school, but . . .

Here, let me imagine a place for you. It's a sort of

circus, a collection of acrobats, jugglers, animal trainers, high-wire artists, clowns, dancers—the whole thing, every kind of performer you'd expect to find in a circus. And this place is parked nearby and it's open round the clock and the idea is anyone can walk in and say to any of these performers, "Hey, I'd like to learn how to do that!" and they say, "Well, of course! That's what we're here for!"

Of course there'd be room here for a lot more. Maybe a small zoo where you could learn to take care of the animals yourself. Maybe somebody would have a pretty good telescope and could show you what's what in the nighttime sky and lend you some books if you're interested. And maybe there'd be a photographer with a bunch of cameras and a darkroom, and somebody with a printing press and a bindery. And while we're at it, why not a weaver and a potter and a sculptor and a painter and a pianist and a violinist, and maybe even someone who knows how to build a piano and how to make a violin? And indeed there would always be building projects under way, so you could learn how to use all the tools and read the blueprints and all that. And someone who was always prepared to take a bunch of kids out into the wilderness to learn whatever there is to learn out there. And maybe an archaeologist who

Here, let me imagine a place for you. It's a sort of circus. . . .

could take some kids off to a dig someplace. And you could even have a writer on hand in case someone was crazy enough to want to find out what that's all about. And a roomful of computers, with someone who knew how to use them. And somewhere in there someone who could teach you any math you wanted to learn, and someone else who could teach you any electronics or physics you wanted to learn, and so on. And gee, everybody has books they can lend you. For your young entrepreneurs, you could even have people around who could help them make and market their products.

Are you getting the idea here? I could go on for hours this way.

Anyway, the rule is, you can come and go as you please, do anything you please, study with anyone you please for as long as you please. How does this sound as someplace you might rather have been than in a classroom? . . .

Exactly, exactly. It'd be a never-ending feast of learning, and if you wanted to keep kids out, you'd have to put up a razor-wire fence. . . .

Oh, well, of course educators would hate it. Educators would be superfluous in such a setup: functionless. They'd say: "Sure, everyone's having a wonderful time, but how do you know they're getting a rounded education?" My answer to that is, "Rounded according to whom?" and "Rounded as of when?" Who says education has to end at age eighteen? Or at age twenty-two? If there were a place like that in my neighborhood, I'd be ensconced there right now, teaching writing, teaching editing, teaching publishing, teaching word processing, teaching everything I have to teach—and learning, getting that "rounded education" I certainly didn't get in sixteen years of schooling. . . .

No, don't call this a school. Didn't you hear what I just said? It isn't a school, it's a city. It's a place where people live who are willing to let their children have access to them. People who are willing to let the children of the community hang around, willing to pay attention to them, willing to talk to them, willing to show them how things work, willing to show them how to do things, willing to let them try out things for themselves. Nothing difficult, nothing very demanding, just the ordinary things people did on this planet for the first three million years of human life.

People in this city wouldn't get as much "done" as people in New York City, wouldn't have as sharp a competitive edge, but they'd have a hell of a lot more fun and they'd find out what it's like to live like human beings instead of workers—and they wouldn't pay a nickel in school taxes. It would be costly in terms of time, of course, but how many hours does the average worker spend right now paying for a system that doesn't work?

Joe Hagan, another SRA alumnus, had been hired as editorial vice president at The Society for Visual Education, which had recently been acquired by the Singer Corporation. SVE had traditionally specialized in audio-visual materials—filmstrips, cassettes, overhead projectuals, and so on. In addition to continuing this supplementary line of materials, Joe wanted to start a new line of multimedia systems designed to support basal curriculum objectives. To give you an example of the difference, the AV side of the company might produce a series of six filmstrips on six key judicial decisions of current importance—*Miranda*, *Roe* v. *Wade*, and so on—which a school might buy for its

AV library and which social studies teachers at various levels might use in any number of contexts. The systems Joe had in mind would be multimedia programs designed to supplement basal school programs. For example, all first-grade teachers have a pretty well-defined set of objectives to meet in mathematics. The materials they're given to work with are almost always printed: textbooks and workbooks. The guides that accompany these materials suggest a myriad of things that'll help: activities, games, and practice materials they can assemble cheaply. Lots of companies offer supplementary materials of various kinds that teachers can buy, often with their own money, but what Joe had in mind was to assemble a complete and completely coordinated supplemental package: filmstrips to introduce basic concepts, taped lessons to reinforce the concepts, games to provide practice with essential skills, and so on. Joe offered me the job of overseeing the development of this product line, with the title of editorial director, and I leaped at it. This was work I was born to do. I understand media and their instructional uses and in the years to follow was surprised to discover how rare a knack this is.

What Joe was offering me was more than work I was born to do. At last I was going to be in a position to decisively affect materials being put into schools by a major educational publisher. And there was more. Joe had accepted his vice presidency with the understanding that the presidency would be his when the present president retired in three years. It was highly likely that, unless I screwed up, I would then move up into Joe's job.

The next three years were tremendously exciting times.

I was doing the best work I'd ever done and was trying to create an environment in which others could do the best work they'd ever done. The products being developed under my direction were a tremendous success—among the most successful in the history of the business, according to Joe. Naturally this was too good to go on for long.

Joe was a bit like me—he had the silly notion that what counts in business is achievement. He had plenty of that to show for his time at SVE; he'd doubled the company's income in three years. But what counts (and is rewarded) in big corporate business is standing in well with the right people, and this Joe had badly neglected, so that when the president retired, the folks at Singer decided they wanted one of their own sort to take that job. For the man they promoted from corporate headquarters, it was just a convenient stepping-stone to greater things. He stayed barely long enough to fire Joe Hagan and install his own editorial vice president (not me, of course).

One day after he'd been in the saddle for about three months, the new president took me aside for a little talk about the stuff I was putting out. "You're making it too good," he told me gravely. "You don't have to make it so good, because it's just for kids, and kids can't tell the difference."

> *"You're making the stuff too good," the president told me gravely.*

I replied in some fashion or other and walked away. This was not an expression of mere philistinism and ignorance on his part. It was an insult to my intelligence. This smoke screen of talk was in fact transparent: He intended to cut my budget, which meant that I would not be *able* to make the products so excessively good. This cut in expenses would produce a pretty little jump in profits, which would make him look good with the folks at the head office. A few days later I sent round my letter of resignation. I could easily have stayed and put up with it (and within two or three years probably been rewarded with a vice presidency), but there are times when one must be a fool for the sake of making a foolish gesture.

I didn't leave bitterly. In fact, I left very well, with a contract to write twelve filmstrips for twenty thousand dollars, almost certainly the highest fee ever paid for a work-for-hire in that medium and industry. It was clearly a sort of golden handshake, though why they thought they owed me one is a mystery. The filmstrips would take about a month to write and storyboard—not bad money for those days (or even these).

This gave us time to set up Daniel Quinn & Associates, a development house, devoted to creating products for educational publishers to publish as their own. It's a feasible business for an aggressive entrepreneur. For someone like me, who is nothing like an aggressive entrepreneur, it's just a sure way to go broke. Nevertheless we did some good things, Rennie and I. Some were still being marketed ten years later. Some are still being marketed today.

One project that was a lot of fun was a set of thirty "read-along" books (books to be read while listening to a taped reading or dramatization of the text) for a publisher in Florida. The objective of the series was to give students the experience of reading as an *enjoyable* activity. (A typically subversive Quinn notion; school people get nervous when their charges start having *fun;* school is supposed to be serious, unpleasant business.) Accordingly, half the series was devoted to genre fiction, which is what most people read for fun: science fiction, mystery, suspense, and even horror. In writing these books, I discovered that (thanks to experience and reading) fiction was no longer a mystery to me.

This project was followed by a lull, which is to say we were out of work. While our sales rep was out trying to find customers for products I'd conceived, I had some time to fiddle with the pieces of a puzzle I'd been shuffling around for the past fifteen years. At this point, I didn't have any idea how they fit together or what they added up to.

When people ask me about the origins of *Ishmael* I usually talk about one or another of the pieces of the puzzle I was exploring.

One was the mystery of how and why we happened to mislay the first three million years of human life. This mystery was composed of several different puzzles. For example, why doesn't human history begin with the birth of humanity? . . .

Ah. Well, of course. That's just my point. History is *defined* so as to begin at a certain arbitrary point, and what came before isn't defined in its own terms but only in terms of its beforeness. It's not history, it's a separate special thing called *prehistory* . . .

No, that's not quite what I'm getting at. Look, let's do this. Let's take all the names you know of literary and dramatic forms of the past and abolish them. I want you to expunge from your memory words like *epic, ballad, saga, tragedy, ode, mystery play, allegory, fable, biography,* and *essay*. I want you to gather them up in your mind and erase them. Okay. Now I'm going to give you a much improved way of thinking about this whole matter of human communications. Television came into being in the late 1940s, as you know. Well, before that there was a long, undifferentiated period of *pre-television*. So, just as you have history and prehistory, now you have television and pre-television.

The key word here is *undifferentiated*. That's what prehistory is. History, by contrast, is a teeming mass of highly differentiated material: movements, leaders, technological and social developments, and so on. Prehistory is simply the great undifferentiated nothingness that existed before history—*our* history—began. This is the universal understanding of how it was. Prehistory was *there;* it went on for a long, long, long time. We all know that. But if you're going to write a text on *history,* if you're going to teach a class on *history,* then you're going to start with something called *the agricultural revolution,* about ten thousand years ago. That, *by definition,* is the beginning of history. For some strange reason, human history doesn't begin with the birth of our species but rather with the birth of a *technology*. Why? How did this very odd state of affairs come to be?

It took me several years to figure it out. When the people of our culture began to have the leisure to wonder about human origins, it never occurred to them to wonder if man had been born anything but an agriculturalist and a civilization-builder. Indeed, why would they? As far as they knew (or could imagine), man was *innately* a farmer and city builder the way that bees are innately honey-gatherers and hive-builders. Thus, for them, agriculture, man, and history all began at the same time, just a few thousand years ago. When Darwin and his followers came along with evidence that man had been born millions of years ago, not thousands, the elegance of this scheme was spoiled, but historians didn't care to give it up. They were used to teaching the story of man as beginning just a few thousand years ago, with the development of agriculture, and they wanted to go on teaching it that way. What difference did it make that man had been around for millions of years? Clearly he wasn't doing anything during this time that was worthy of the notice of *historians*. The historians therefore washed their hands of it and turned it over to archaeologists to think about. Historians stuck to history, and they stuck to their ancient definition of it as beginning just a few thousand years ago, with the very special agricultural revolution that marks the birth of our culture.

> *When Darwin came along, the elegance of the ancient scheme of history was spoiled, but historians didn't care to give it up.*

In his autobiography, Malcolm X said that at one point the role of the white race in human history came to him with great clarity: The white race is Satan. I was very struck with this way of thinking about things, though I knew that his identification was not a good mythological fit. Satan is inherently an outsider—the common enemy of mankind, to be hated and feared as much by white people as by any other. His objectives are spiritual and otherworldly, totally unlike those of the white race. We didn't go to Africa to turn the natives into sinners, we went there to turn them into slaves. Satan isn't interested in wealth, territory, or temporal power—and the white race is interested in almost nothing else. Nevertheless, I had the feeling that Malcolm was onto something.

A few years before, I'd had an illuminating conversation with a young black man I met at a private sale of African art. He'd come to the sale more or less out of curiosity and didn't know what to make of the things he was seeing. He was startled when I told him most of them were fakes—fakes in the sense that they'd been made for export rather than for tribal use. In effect, they were just a fair grade of tourist goods. He asked how I knew this, and I had to think about it. How *did* I know it? There's a profound difference between a piece of work that is strange to our eyes but fresh and beautiful and lively, and a piece of work that is strange to our eyes but crudely wrought and ugly and lifeless. He'd come expecting to see "primitive art" and it all looked equally "primitive" to him, and I had to show him how to see it in a new way —how to see it the way the artist saw it, how to "think primitive." I was in the odd position of revealing to him the values of his own heritage, which white culture had taught him to despise.

One thing led to another. Finally, deciding I could be trusted with this secret, he confessed to me that he didn't really understand how *all this* had come about and how it fit together. He knew, of course, that there were prehistoric times and Stone Age peoples, but . . . where had it all started and how had it gotten to be like this? Talking to him—and he was not an uneducated person—I realized that this uncertainty about the fundamental outlines of the human story must be very widespread. I couldn't imagine—can't imagine—anything sadder than a whole sapient, conscious race of people being unable to pass on to their children even the crudest understanding of their own origins.

When people ask about the origins of *Ishmael*, I tell this story, as I tell the story of Malcolm identifying the white race as Satan. I tell this one as well. At that time Erich von Däniken was minting money with a book called *Chariots of the Gods?*, in which he proposed that alien astronauts were responsible not only for building the pyramids and all the wonders of the ancient world but for producing the human race itself, by kindly condescending to interbreed with our apelike ancestors. It isn't enough to say that only very gullible people would swallow such nonsense; profound ignorance is required as well. The gullible millions who swallowed von Däniken's proposal would not have swallowed the proposal that alien astronauts were responsible for building the *Queen Mary* and Hoover Dam.

It seemed to me it would be a wonderfully rewarding

> *It would be a wonderfully rewarding task to produce a telling of the human story that would dispel the lie that human life was meaningless except for the last half of one percent of it.*

task to produce a telling of the human story that would be a healing of that story. A telling that would dispel the lie that human life was meaningless except for the last half of one percent of it. A telling that would enable that young African American to perceive our *common* roots in the human story. A telling that would show why our ancestors needed no help from ersatz gods in UFOs to become human or to produce wonders that are still wonders today.

But I had other objectives as well.

The songs of the sixties and early seventies had warned that a hard rain was gonna fall and that the times they were a-changin', but I had little hope that these things were going to happen in fact. The kids had lots of slogans, but a revolution needs more than that. A revolution needs a brilliant new vision and a foundation to build on, and these things the kids had not. They had no *text,* such as idealists of the past century had found in the *Communist Manifesto.* The revolution was going to fail in this generation, but I felt sure that the conditions that had stimulated the desire for revolution were not going to go away —worse luck for us. The day would come in twenty years or fifty years when children would again stand up and say, "No more, we've had enough of this." And this time I wanted them to have a text *in hand,* ready for use.

These were the ideas and ambitions that were chasing themselves around in my head in that spring of 1977 as I sat down to start a book called *Man and Alien,* a book I thought would keep me busy for six months and ended up keeping me busy for the better part of twelve years.

There was one other matter at the back of my mind—as it had been for the past twenty years. I was still looking for a way to understand what had happened to me that morning at Gethsemani. Though I was by now for all practical purposes an atheist, I knew I'd never be able to dismiss or deny this experience—or to forget it.

ELEVEN

Thinkers of the Abrahamic religious tradition —Jews, Christians, and Muslims—have always been prepared to find God in human history. Naturally, this means the abbreviated form of human history that was known when these religions came into being. In each of the religions of this tradition, it was understood that man (and indeed the world) was only a few thousand years old. This was the foundation: Man was born a few thousand years ago, immediately fell from grace, and began to build civilization. This was the history in which they expected to find God and did indeed find God.

When Darwin and his successors made it clear that man is millions of years older than this history, the thinkers of these religions at first perceived this as a crisis. Some still do perceive it as a crisis and reject all evidence of human antiquity, but most found another way to deal with the crisis. They ignored it. They agreed to pretend that it never happened. This worked very well for them. Least said, soonest mended.

History, philosophy, and religion joined hands on this issue. They had all come into being accepting a premise that seemed almost self-evident: Man was inherently an agriculturalist and a civilization-builder, just the way bees are inherently honey-collectors and hive-builders, and this meant he was just a few thousand years old. They had all grown to maturity with these notions at the base of all their reasoning and all their conclusions, and none of them, here at this late date, wanted to shake the foundations on which their sacred institutions were built. History, philosophy, and religion therefore joined hands and said—quietly but firmly—"The first three million years of human life are meaningless. They're there, but we're not going to look at them or think about them, because they were *empty.* Truly human life, the human life that *counts,* began just a few thousand years ago, and we will concern ourselves with no other."

The God of the Abrahamic tradition began to concern himself in the affairs of men just a few thousand years ago. Before that, we must assume, he was occupied elsewhere. Or perhaps he looked down on our ancestors and said, "Yech! What lowbrows! I snub them! I will have nothing to do with them." He turned up his nose at *Homo habilis,* at *Homo erectus,* and even at *Homo sapiens* for hundreds of thousand of years. Even *Homo sapiens sapiens* he wouldn't touch at first: Ten thousand generations of people every bit as smart as you or I went down to death ignored by God. But finally, just a few centuries ago, God looked down on man and said, "At last man is worthy of my attention. For three million years, I have let him welter in ignorance, error, and despair, but now I'll begin to talk to him."

Well, of course, I began by rejecting this priggish god. I went beyond that. I refused to concede that the singularity of this priggish god made him morally superior to all others. Looking at the universe, I find nothing in it that indicates the numerosity of the divine. Atheists claim to know the number of the gods; they say that number is zero. Monotheists also claim to know the number of the gods; they say that number is one. I personally don't know the number of the gods and don't know where to look for it. It doesn't trouble me to be ignorant of this number; I'm even comfortable with the notion that it may be zero. The presence of the divine in the universe doesn't necessarily depend on or argue for the presence of gods.

> *Like the thinkers of the Abrahamic tradition, I too expected to find the gods in human history—but in the whole of it, not just in the last tenth of one percent of it.*

But I was like the thinkers of the Abrahamic tradition in one respect: I too expected to find the gods in human history—but in the whole of it, not just in the last tenth of one percent of it. But how was I to look for them? Where was I to look for them? They were certainly not to be found in what occultists call the Old Gods, the pagan gods. Those gods are not old at all, are scarcely older than Yahweh; these are farmers' gods one and all, gods of the fields and the orchards, gods of fertility, gods whose birth and death foreshadow the growth and harvest of the crops. I wasn't looking for Osiris and Astarte and Adonis. The gods I sought were unknown, would not have been imaginable (much less nameable) to our earliest human ancestors.

I won't lead you step by agonizing step to the realization that I'd been given a compass to use in the search. It had two points to fix its direction, as a compass must if it's to be usable. One of these was my childhood dream, which had directed me firmly toward the community of life. The other was of course that hour at Gethsemani, which, like the invisible magnet of the north pole, pulled me forward with a wordless message so completely unrelated to the monastic life or to the Christian life or to Jesus or perfection or holiness or heaven that I couldn't begin to make it out till I'd rid myself of all that impedimenta and was ready to step off the sidewalk and follow the deer into the forest. . . .

I understand. You'd like to know what was said, even if it wasn't said in words. I'll do the best I can. It was something like this: *I am the fire of life that animates the world. I am not to be found in the sky, not to be found in some remote heaven. I live in your midst, and all that lives lives in the midst of me. I am HERE and I am never absent.*

I apologize that I'm unable to infuse those words with

the thunderous emotions I felt. I produced something more satisfactory in a kind of canticle or paean that I wrote for the fourth version of the book, *The Book of Nahash*. When you leave, I'll give you a copy to take with you. . . . No, it's not a prayer. Gods like these don't need prayers or praise or adoration, and we can't buy their patronage with such things. . . .

I understand. In the case of this hour at Gethsemani, why did I say that "the god spoke" instead of "the gods"? I speak of "the god" in this case because—I lament the fact that English has no genderless personal pronoun. To hell with it, I'll call it *it*. This was not a divine chorus chanting in the sky. This was the god of that particular place. This god was *there*. This was not a god whose home was in the clouds or beyond the stars. This was a god whose home was in the hills of Kentucky. Nowhere else in the universe will you find that place. It's the place that has been shaped by that god. Or that place *is* that god. The fire that animates that place, unique in all the universe, is the god who spoke to me that day, is the god who let me watch it *breathing* that place.

The god who animates that place is not the god who animates Great Bear Lake or the prairie of southern Illinois or the Black Forest or the Greenland tundra or the Kalahari Desert. This is not a generic god, not an abstraction of divinity. Aboriginal peoples everywhere understand this, because they too are *there*.

I'm getting ahead of myself, but I have to say this before you leave: The gods are not invulnerable or all-powerful just because they're gods. The association of omnipotence with divinity is just a lunatic notion that grew up among a people obsessed with power. Drop a nuclear bomb on those hills in Kentucky, and the god of that place will be *silent*. I assure you of that.

The god of this place, Austin, isn't dead or even injured. Even in cities, humans do not constitute an alien presence on this planet. There's room for us here. One of the nice things about Austin is that its citizens don't want to kill off the god who animates this place (though of course they don't think of it in these terms).

Now, where was I? I was in search of the gods. . . .

Having listened to the god in the hills of Kentucky, I knew that it wasn't burning there just for *us*. Fifty thousand years ago, when this continent was uninhabited by our kind, this god was there, burning with not one whit less exuberance and joy than today. What I perceived that day was the overwhelming preciousness of life and the laughable insignificance of the things we humans puff ourselves up over. Theologians of the school of Teilhard de Chardin conceive that the universe yearns to be "hominized" and so turned a great corner when man was born. In us, as they see it, the universe became *conscious*. This is rather like thinking that, when Edmund Hillary stood on top of it, Mount Everest became *tall*. Standing in the midst of those hills charged and thrumming with the divine fire, I knew that the world needs our consciousness the way the sun needs a kitchen match. But, because consciousness is peculiar to humans, we like to think it's the most valuable treasure in the cosmos; if birds were capable of self-congratulation of this sort, doubtless they'd think the same about flight, or perhaps about bird-song. I don't mean to imply that consciousness *isn't* a treasure. It's *all* a treasure: the flight of the bird, the stride of the cheetah, the song of the whale, the web of the spider, the veins of a leaf. But to nominate consciousness as something grander than all the rest is just more of the usual anthropocentric nonsense. . . .

Ah. Yes, that's a valid point. In *Ishmael* I argued the necessity of giving other species the time and room to reach for consciousness. Indeed we must. But I certainly didn't mean to recommend a special dispensation for creatures with the potential for consciousness. I didn't mean that we should protect gorillas more carefully than squids. We must give every species the time and the room to reach *whatever* potential it possesses. To do otherwise is to pre-empt the wisdom of the gods, is to exercise the knowledge of good and evil that was forbidden to Adam. . . .

> *Having listened to the god in the hills of Kentucky, I knew that it wasn't burning there just for us.*

Ah yes, our "stewardship." People with good intentions often tell me we have an obligation to be "good stewards" of the earth. I must ask, who gave us this stewardship? Those who believe Genesis contains actual words spoken by God will say He gave us this stewardship when the earth was created, and I wouldn't dream of arguing with them. But people who know that the earth got along just fine without man for three billion years have no such excuse for believing in our stewardship, which is again nothing but arrogance and vanity and anthropocentric tomfoolery. We have as much business being stewards of the world as infants have being stewards of the nursery. It's we who are dependent on the world, not the other way round.

Following the arrow of my compass, I went back to our beginnings to find meaning that historians and philosophers and theologians say is not there. Let me read to you from the fifth version of the book, *The Book of the Damned*. Here the people of our culture are identified as a new, self-defined subspecies of man called *Homo magister*—Man the Master. I never found a way to say it better than this:

When *Homo magister* looks at the history of our ancient ancestors, he naturally perceives it as a void, as non-history. How else can you characterize it, except as what was going on before anything happened? It's just before-history. Prehistory. It's a period of time as empty as the lives that created it. It's empty because nobody was doing anything. Except hunting and gathering. And of course battering stones. It was the Stone Age. Definition by product.

Homo magister would naturally see it that way. But it's not the only way to see it. Be imaginative. Forget products. Forget occupations. Imagine it a different way.

Imagine that our ancestors were enacting a story.

You know what enacting a story is. We're enacting a story here. A story about man becoming the master of his environment. A story about man's conquest of the world. A story about the fulfillment of man's destiny—

as defined by *Homo magister*. We've been enacting that story for some ten thousand years.

Imagine our ancestors enacting a different story from ours. Not a story about man mastering his environment. Not a story about man's conquest of the world. Not a story in which products and productivity figured at all.

Stretch yourself. Imagine that the story our ancestors were enacting *shaped their lives*. The way the story we're enacting shapes *our* lives.

Different stories: different lives.

Imagine that their lives had a different shape from ours because they were enacting a different story from ours.

Go further. Imagine that enacting their story made their lives meaningful to them. The way that enacting our story makes our lives meaningful to us.

> *Imagine that our ancestors' lives had a different shape from ours because they were enacting a different story from ours.*

Different stories: different meanings.

Imagine that enacting their story, generation after generation, gave their history its shape. The way that enacting our story, generation after generation, has given our history its shape.

Different stories: different histories.

Imagine that their history had a different shape from ours because they were enacting a different story from ours.

It's hard, I know, to imagine such things. It'd be like asking an eighteenth-century slave-ship captain to imagine that the wretches chained up in his hold were actually human beings like himself, like his wife, like his parents. He'd have thought you were pulling his leg.

It gets worse.

Think biologically. Imagine a completely different kind of story from the one we're enacting. A story for the entire lifetime of a genus. The genus *Homo*. Think of an outline for such a story. Not three million years of nothingness, followed by an explosive flourishing so violent that it consumes the world in ten thousand years, followed by extinction. That's not a story for the lifetime of a genus.

Imagine a different story entirely. A story for tens of millions of years. For hundreds of millions of years.

A real story. A story to be enacted. A story whose enactment shapes the history of those who enact it. Now imagine that that's the story our ancestors were enacting. It had nothing to do with mastering the world. Nobody was trying to master the world. All of it was about something else.

Stretch yourself.

Imagine that during the first three million years of human life people were enacting a story. And that it was man's destiny to enact that story. Not for three million years. For thirty million years. For three hundred million years. For the lifetime of our planet, perhaps. Billions of years.

It was that good a story. Good enough for the lifetime of a genus. But it was not a story about power— about conquest and mastery and ruling. Enacting it didn't make people powerful. Enacting it, people didn't need to be powerful. Because, enacting it, people didn't need to rule the world.

Imagine that ruling the world was something they thought they didn't need to do. Because it was *already being done*. As it had always been done. As it had been done from the beginning.

Imagine that they had a different supposition about the world and man's place in it. Imagine that they didn't suppose, as *Homo magister* does, that the world belongs to man, that it is his to conquer and rule. Imagine that, in their ignorance, they supposed something else entirely.

Be outrageous.

Imagine that they supposed something completely absurd. That *man belongs to the world*.

It was never hidden. It was only hidden from *Homo magister* because he was sure that what had shaped their lives was *nothing*—an absence of knowledge, ignorance.

> *Imagine that ruling the world was something they thought they didn't need to do. Because it was* already being done.

Not *something*. Not a different supposition about the world and man's place in it.

Man belongs to the world.

Actually, it's plainly written in their lives. It's plainly written in the general community to which they belonged: the community of life on this planet. Anyone can read it. You just have to look.

Every creature born in the biological community of the earth *belongs* to that community. Nothing lives in isolation from the rest; nothing *can* live in isolation from the rest. Nothing lives only *in* itself, needing nothing *from* the community. Nothing lives only *for* itself, owing nothing *to* the community. Nothing is untouchable or untouched. Every life in the community is owed to the community—and is paid back to the community in death. The community is a web of life, and every strand of the web is a path to all the other strands. Nothing is exempt. Nothing is special. Nothing lives on a strand by itself, unconnected to the rest.

Nothing is wasted.

Everything that lives is food for another. And everything that feeds is ultimately itself fed upon or in death returns its substance to the community. And in belonging to the community, each species is shaped. By belonging.

By belonging, by feeding and being fed upon, each generation of each species is shaped. Of each generation, some, better suited to survive, live to reproduce. Others, not as well suited, do not.

And so the generations are shaped. By belonging to the community that shapes them.

Nothing is exempt from the shaping.

The fishes that, four hundred million years ago, lived in the offshore shallows of the oceans were shaped. And learned to venture up onto the land. And in venturing onto the land were shaped by their contact with the community already living there. And some were shaped in such a way that, over millions of years, they became reptiles. No longer tied to the shore, the reptiles ventured inland.

Where they were shaped.

So that some of them, shaped in one way, became birds. So that others of them, shaped in other ways, became mammals. And the mammals, belonging to a community of plants, birds, amphibians, and reptiles, were shaped. Into many different forms. Into rodents and bats and anteaters and dogs and horses and deer and elephants and apes.

And all of these were shaped. By belonging to the community of life. By feeding and being fed upon.

And, over millions of years, the members of one branch of the family of apes were shaped into a manlike creature we call *Australopithecus africanus*. And *Australopithecus africanus* was shaped over millions of years until he became *Australopithecus robustus*—stronger and taller and more manlike, until, looking at him, we have to call him . . . man. *Homo habilis*.

Man was born belonging to the world. Being shaped. And, being shaped, *Homo habilis* became stronger and taller and more dexterous and more intelligent, until, looking at him, we have to give him a new name: *Homo erec-*

Man was born belonging to the world. Being shaped.

tus. And *Homo erectus* was born being shaped, and he belonged to the community that was shaping him. His *life* belonged to that community. And those of each generation who were less well suited to survive in the community rendered back their lives at an early age, while the rest lived on to reproduce. And so *Homo erectus* was shaped, so that he became stronger, taller, more agile, more dexterous, and more intelligent, until, looking at him, we have to call him *us* . . . *Homo sapiens*. And *Homo sapiens* was born being shaped. He was born a member of the community that was shaping him. Not exempt from membership by virtue of his greater intelligence. Not isolated from the rest by virtue of his capacity to wonder and dream. Not aloof from the rest by virtue of his knowing that he was unlike the rest in these ways. He was a part of the rest.

And being a part of the rest, *Homo sapiens* was shaped. Shaped not by nothing. Shaped not by ignorance. Shaped by belonging to the community of life. Which was itself being shaped. The community itself was being shaped. The matter was being handled.

Not by man. The shaping of the world was not in man's hands. It was in other hands, which had shaped it from the beginning. It was in the hands of the gods.

The gods were shaping the community of life on earth. And man belonged to that community and was being shaped with it and in it. Man was being shaped by the gods. Man was living in the hands of the gods. And the gods did not rebuke him. Or send him teachers. Or send him saviors. Because there was no need to. Because he was living in their hands.

Man had found his destiny. He had been fulfilling it from the beginning. It was his destiny to live in the hands of the gods. For the lifetime of this planet.

Because no theologian of the Abrahamic tradition had ever dared to see if God had been present in the human story from the beginning, none had ever understood what the Fall was about. What Adam threw away wasn't heaven (heaven isn't even mentioned in the story), it was life— life in the hands of the gods for the lifetime of this planet.

It had taken me five years to get all the pieces of the puzzle together. The knowledge of good and evil is the knowledge the gods use to rule the world, so-called because every single thing they do is good for some and evil for others. This is plainly the knowledge that the people of our culture have been exercising in the world since we began to take it over, starting some ten thousand years ago. Every morning the people of our culture shake the sleep out of their heads and reach for the fruit of that tree, the Tree of the Knowledge of Good and Evil. Every morning they roll out of bed and proclaim themselves ready and competent to rule the world in the place of the gods.

As the authors of Genesis tell the story, God said to Adam, "You may eat of any tree you find in the garden, except that one. For if you eat of that one, you'll die." He wasn't speaking of the death of an individual but of Adam, the race of man itself. And that's what we're facing here as we celebrate ten thousand years of running the world: wholesale slaughter of the community of life, relentless destruction of our environment, and human extinction.

After five years, having learned to become my own teacher, I found myself in possession of a new vision of human history and a new understanding of the spiritual catastrophe identified in religious tradition as the Fall. Another seven years would pass before I found a way to bring them together in a book.

> *Because no theologian of the Abrahamic tradition had ever dared to see if God had been present in the human story from the beginning, none had ever understood what the Fall was about.*

TWELVE

If tomorrow we were to wake up and learn that the night had brought forth a new, vital religion so universally acceptable to humanity that all religious disagreement had utterly vanished from the world, this would be accounted one of the greatest miracles in history and the very greatest miracle in the history of our spiritual development.

Well, there once was such a religion on this planet. Everyone is more or less aware of this fact, but no one—no one at all—has ever suggested that this was miraculous or even remarkable. No one has ever suggested that this universal religion might have even the slightest claim to validity. Needless to say, this was not one of *our* religions. It was (and is) the religion of the Leavers,* and for this reason it is judged not to count as a religion at all, is judged to be merely a pre-religion, a crude evolutionary stage that people had to pass through in order to arrive at the enlightened and advanced religions that evoke such murderous fervor among the Takers.†

I don't imagine you know the name of this once-universal religion. It's animism, the only world religion whose name you needn't bother to capitalize. It isn't a name coined by any adherent of this religion. Who would bother to ask a savage to supply a name? Derived from the Latin word for soul or spirit, in the 1860s and 1870s it came to be applied to the religious notions of primitive peoples. An early definition was supplied by Sir Edward Tyler in his book *Primitive Culture:*

> Animism is the doctrine which places the sources of mental and even physical life in an energy independent of, or at least distinct from, the body. From the point of view of the history of religions, the term is taken, in the wider sense, to denote the belief in the existence of spiritual beings, some attached to bodies of which they constitute the real personality (souls), others without necessary connection with a determinate body (spirits).

Simply put, as it's understood by Taker scholars, animism represents spirit worship as opposed to the presumably more advanced worship of gods or God. In other words

---

* In *Ishmael,* "those who leave the rule of the world in the hands of the gods" (in other words, "primitive" peoples).

† In *Ishmael,* "those who have taken the rule of the world into their own hands" (in other words, the people of our "advanced" culture).

(as it is imagined), these poor, benighted savages have the silly idea that every tree and bush and rock "has a spirit in it." This is what makes it a "pre-religion"; true religions are concerned with gods, not spirits. Considering the unbridled anthropocentrism of the Taker mentality, it isn't hard to figure out why this should be so: Gods are like *us* (which makes them preeminently deserving of worship).

A spirit in a tree is a what? It doesn't have a name, you can't talk to it or expect it to talk back to you. It's just there. Gods have personality, just like us. Gods have personal lives, just like us. Gods have gender, sex lives, and even babies, just like us. They visit the earth and talk to people (who else would they talk to?), get involved in our lives. They listen to our troubles, take sides in our quarrels, look after us on our journeys, see that our enterprises get a little help, and so on. I speak here of the Olympian gods, the gods of pagan Greece and Rome.

> *The only universal religion the world has ever known is judged to be merely a pre-religion, a crude evolutionary stage that people had to get past.*

Of course, having just a single god is considered to be even more advanced. The bad part about having just one god, however, is that it can only be one sex or the other, which puts it in the middle of the war of the sexes. If it's a he, it tends to see things from the male point of view, and if it's a she it tends to see things from the female point of view. The current controversy over God's sex doesn't strike anyone as being the least bit primitive. If God is going to be like us, then there must be sexual equipment of one kind or the other, even though it presumably doesn't get much use.

In his own way, the god of the Abrahamic tradition is even more anthropomorphic than the Olympian gods. He loves us, talks to us, listens to us, gives us gifts, takes them back, frames laws for our conduct, gets angry when we fail to obey them, punishes us, forgives us, keeps track of our every thought throughout our lives, and at death rewards us with everlasting bliss or damnation. (He isn't as big on damnation as he used to be; in some of the more advanced religions, he has quietly closed down hell and boarded it up like a decrepit amusement park.) All these things are clear indicators that one is dealing with an advanced religion, a religion worthy of the name. It is not thought to be the least superstitious to believe that God has an especially keen interest in what people get up to in their bedrooms.

As I say, the religion of the Leavers is "pre" because it doesn't involve the worship of anthropomorphic gods like these. You'll find plenty of gods in their mythologies, of course, but these are only local deities—not objects of universal worship or even of local worship, as we use the term. For example, the Amazulu of Africa say that Unkulunkulu made all things, but they don't worship this creator the way Jews worship Yahweh or the way Christians worship Jesus. And if the Amazulu were to run across a band of Ashanti, they wouldn't expect them to acknowledge the primacy of Unkulunkulu over their Onyankopon. You see what I mean; this is a sign of their religious backwardness. If the Amazulu were instead to fall upon the Ashanti and slaughter them for refusing to acknowledge the primacy of Unkulunkulu, this would represent a clear step forward on the path of spiritual development, and we'd be forced to acknowledge that the Amazulu now had a true religion.

While on (or near) the subject of anthropomorphism, I should point out that, when I say that a god spoke to me that day in Kentucky, I use these words in a completely metaphorical way. Nothing spoke—and certainly no one spoke. I didn't experience the presence of a person at all. The world was ablaze with a divine fire. That's what I experienced, and the rest is just my struggle to find some words that will help you understand what I experienced and what I later understood from the experience.

> *If the Amazulu were to fall upon the Ashanti and slaughter them, then we'd acknowledge that the Amazulu had a true religion.*

Animism is the only world religion that has never been named or defined by its own adherents. It's the only world religion that has never generated a sacred foundation text; it's hard to imagine how it could have done, since it was never the religion of a single nation or people. It's probably just as well. When you have a text, you almost inevitably have schisms and heretics, divisions by interpretations and divisions by degrees of orthodoxy. All the same, it makes it difficult to answer people's questions.

———

A few weeks ago an *Ishmael* reader by the name of Judith phoned me. Conversations with Judith can be disconcerting, because she has the unique knack of asking questions that knock me off my center of balance, so that I topple in some new and unexpected direction. She wasn't even aware of having this ability until I pointed it out and is as puzzled by it as I am. On this occasion she said, "Daniel, I'm calling to see if you have any tapes of the meetings you've had with groups about *Ishmael.*"

I said, "Well, I haven't made any as yet, though I know I should have. What are you looking for in particular?"

"I've given *Ishmael* to several people at my church, including the minister, and they feel rather at sea. They have questions they'd like to ask, but you're four hundred miles away. I thought maybe if you had a tape I could give them . . ."

"This is too bad. A couple weeks ago I had a six-hour conference with about twenty-five priests, ministers, rabbis, and other assorted clergy in California. I should definitely have taped that."

"You certainly should have. What was it about?"

"That's a good question. The rabbi who organized the event said everyone in the group had read the book and felt very 'challenged' by it. But what they wanted to talk to me about I didn't know until I got there."

"You went to California without knowing what you were going there for?"

I thought about that for a bit, then asked: "If I flew up to Oklahoma to talk to the people at your church, would I know what I was going there for?"

"No, I suppose not. I see what you mean. So what did they want?"

"It was really quite astonishing. They wanted to know how to reconcile their faiths with what they'd read in *Ishmael*."

"It wasn't the other way around?"

"No, it wasn't. They weren't challenging me to defend *Ishmael*. On the contrary, they were saying, 'It seems to us that in writing *Ishmael* you have undermined our beliefs. If this isn't the case, please show us why.'"

"Wow. What did you say?"

"I'm afraid I waffled shamelessly. It gives me no joy to be responsible for people losing their faith. No, that's not quite accurate. I very much want to be responsible for people looking at their old ethnocentric and anthropocentric beliefs and saying, 'Good lord, this is gibberish. I see that now.' Two very different things are involved here. Many people have written to me to say, 'You've shattered my beliefs—and I thank you for it!' That's very gratifying. But I don't like hearing from people who say, 'You've shattered my beliefs. Does that mean I have to give them up?' It's pro-

> *I want people to look at their old ethnocentric and anthropocentric beliefs and say, "Good lord, this is gibberish."*

foundly alien to my nature to decide what people should believe. That's something Takers consider themselves divinely qualified to do, but I don't."

"Even so," Judith said, "don't you feel an obligation of some kind to your readers?"

"What kind of obligation do you mean?"

"I mean, how can you shatter people's beliefs and just walk away?"

"I haven't walked away, I'm right here. What do you want from me?"

"I want some guidance. These people here that I told you about—they also want some guidance."

"What kind of guidance?"

"You could start by telling us what you replaced your own shattered beliefs with. After reading *Ishmael* half a dozen times, I just can't believe you're the sort of person who can go through life without a spiritual vision of the universe."

"You're right, of course. I never tried to pretend otherwise."

"Well, why won't you share that vision with us? Why are you keeping it to yourself?"

"Well, Judith, to tell you the plain, dumb truth, it never occurred to me to share it. I wasn't being selfish, I was just being discreet. I don't like pushing my views on other people."

"You don't have to push them. Just give us access to them."

I promised I'd try to find a way to do that. I hope I've made at least a beginning at it here.

It's true I'm uneasy in the role of prophet, not from

any sense of modesty or unworthiness. A teacher, yes: One who says, "Take a look at this and this and this and this. Now, having done so, don't you find the following conclusion to be irresistible?" I'm less comfortable in the posture of one who says, "Here, take my word for this. Don't listen to others, listen only to me."

Another great supporter of *Ishmael* sent me a book called *Disappointment with God* and asked me what I thought of it. As the title suggests, it's a study of people's disappointment with God: Why did God let this terrible thing happen? Why didn't God respond to my prayers? And so on. I found it puzzling that he'd want my opinion of it, but by the time I was finished I realized that the book had given me an insight into my own relationship to the universe: I am never disappointed with God (or as I prefer to say, the gods). This is because I never expect the gods to take my side against others. If I come down with the flu, I don't expect the gods to take my side against the virus that is pursuing its life in my body. If I travel to Africa, I don't expect the gods to strike dead a mosquito that is about to have lunch on my neck (and incidentally give me a case of malaria). If a wildcat attacks me in the hills of New Mexico, I don't expect the gods to help me kill it. If I'm swimming in the ocean, I don't expect the

> *I am never disappointed with the gods, because I never expect them to take my side against others.*

gods to chase away the sharks. I have no illusion that the gods favor me (or any other human) over viruses, sharks, wildcats, mosquitos, or any other life form. And if they don't favor me over a june bug or a mushroom, why would they favor me over another human being? If a friend of mine is killed in a random act of terrorist violence, I'm not going to blame the gods for this. To me, this would be nonsense. And I certainly don't expect the gods to suspend the laws of physics to protect me from landslides, lightning bolts, or burning buildings.

Don't misunderstand me. The fact that the gods don't take our side against others doesn't imply that we have to do the same. The horse doesn't wait for the gods to intervene when it's attacked by a puma; it uses all its strength and every weapon it possesses to save its life. We're free to do the same—as free as any other creature. If a lion attacks us, the gods will not defend us, because they're no more on our side than they are on the side of the lion, but we're at liberty to defend ourselves with whatever weapon we can wield. Our best weapon of defense is of course our intelligence. If there's a cancer growing inside of you, the gods aren't on your side against it, but that doesn't mean you have to throw up your hands and allow it to destroy your life; defend yourself against it with every resource you can bring to bear.

People have written to me to ask: "What can I do about the spiders that invade my house? May I kill them or do I just have to put up with them?" Such questions can always be safely referred to our neighbors in the community of life. A dog or a chimpanzee or a sparrow cannot be mistaken in such matters; they cannot mislead themselves with false, convenient arguments. Ask your dog what he does with the fleas that invade his coat, and he'll show you: He does his best to rid himself of them. You can do the same, without apology. The gods will not take your side against the rest of the world just because you're human, but they will also not take the side of the rest of the world against you just because you're human.

As you see, the so-called Problem of Evil doesn't exist for me. As I explained in *Ishmael*, what the gods know about good and evil is this: Whatever they do is good for one but evil for another, and it can't be otherwise. If the quail eats the grasshopper, then this is good for the quail but evil for the grasshopper. And if the fox eats the quail, then this is good for the fox but evil for the quail. The gods obviously can't make a rule like "No quail may eat a grasshopper" or "Quails deserve to be protected from foxes." Grasshopper, quail, and fox all live in the hands of the gods for a time, and not one of them has cause for complaint or disappointment. The same is true of us. As I said in *The Book of the Damned*, "Every life in the community is owed to the community—and is paid back to the community in death. The community is a web of life, and every strand of the web is a path to all the other strands. Noth-

Most Takers are terrified of death. To die is considered a great tragedy.

ing is exempt. Nothing is special. Nothing lives on a strand by itself, unconnected to the rest." This applies to us as well.

Most Takers are terrified of death. To die is considered a great tragedy among them. They're terrified of it because they've worked so hard to distance themselves from it, to eliminate it from their lives. (To eliminate it as a firsthand experience, I mean; they love to experience it vicariously, sitting in front of their television sets.) When I say that they work hard to distance themselves from death, I don't mean from their own mortality. They distance themselves from that too, of course, but that's not what I'm talking about.

People who live in close contact with the community of life also live in close contact with death. To forestall your immediate first thought, I'm not saying that this makes them insensitive to it. Quite the opposite; they're more sensitive to death than we are, because they see very clearly, every single day, that the life that flows through them is taken from the creatures around them; it comes from nowhere else. If they're to live, others must die. This isn't peculiar to them, this is true of every creature in the community of life (green plants excepted, of course). When we (who distance ourselves as far as possible from the general community of life) open up a frozen dinner and stick it in the microwave, we're totally unconscious of the fact that the life we derive from this meal originally belonged to others. It's quite different for the hunters who carry a deer back to camp. They knew this creature in life, and they know that they took its life so that they and their families could live. They know very well that, in consuming the deer, they're taking the life of the deer into themselves. In fact, in a very real sense, the deer hasn't died at all; the deer has simply become them, and in the same sense they have become the deer. Long before we did, the ancient hunters knew that you are what you eat.

When the hunter takes the life of a deer, this is not a crime or an act of cruelty. That deer is on its way to becoming a human being. And if the hunter should fall prey to a lion, then that hunter is on his way to becoming a lion. The entire community is woven together in this way. Everything that lives has its life from others; there is no other way to get it (unless you happen to be a green plant, as I say). Everything that dies is life for some other —every single thing.

I should add that this is just as true for vegetarians as for anyone else. Vegetarians who feel morally superior because they never eat animals are exhibiting what might be called *kingdomism,* in effect assigning a greater sacredness to members of their own kingdom (the animal kingdom) than to the plant kingdom. As the animist sees the world, everything that lives is sacred, the carrot no less than the cow. If there is any single doctrine that might win universal agreement among animists, I think it would be this, that the gods love everything that lives and have no favorites. If the gods have as much care for me as they do for a dandelion or a dragonfly, I'm perfectly content.

Perhaps the best words I ever wrote outside of *Ishmael* were these in *The Book of Nahash:*

To each is given its moment in the blaze, its spark to be surrendered to another when it is sent, so that the blaze may go on. None may deny its spark to the general blaze and live forever. Each is sent to another someday. You are sent; you are on your way. I am sent. To the wolf or the lion or the vulture or the grasses, I am sent. My death is the life of another, and I will stand again in the windswept grasses and look through the eyes of the fox and take the air with the eagle and run in the track of the deer.

What? Do I consider myself an animist? Yes, I suppose so, but what does this mean? I don't go to an animist church or say animist prayers or vote the animist ticket or try to convert people to animism. All these things are foreign to the animist sensibility. No one can stand up and say (truthfully), "I am the Animist-in-Chief of the world, and only I am empowered to speak for it." No ritual is needed to make you an animist if you wish to become one. There is no animist creed to which all animists subscribe, no animist theology that articulates the nature of the gods, no animist catechism that will supply answers to all questions. I suppose such things could be trumped up by somebody. If people can make money off shamanism, I'm sure they can figure out a way of making money off animism as well.

> *To each is given its moment in the blaze, its spark to be surrendered to another when it is sent, so that the blaze may go on.*

Animism isn't a collection of practices and doctrines that are drawn upon for special occasions. It isn't an aspect of life that can be separated out and isolated from all others. Animists are not so much people with a religion as people with a fundamentally religious way of looking at things. This is not at all to say that animists are uniformly saints—kindly, sweet, gentle, and so on; this is as great a distortion as to say that they're uniformly savages—bloodthirsty, cruel, murderous, and so on. The Iroquois were animists, but (by most civilized standards) they were not nice folks. I recommend the film *Black Robe* to people who imagine that all Leavers are saints (or who imagine that I'm saying that all Leavers are saints). What I said in *Ishmael* stands: There is no One Right Way to live. What we find among Leaver peoples is that each has a way that works well for them. We may not like one particular way, we may think it atrocious and cruel, but it's their way, not ours, and the most murderous culture in human history is hardly in a position to set itself up as the moral policeman of the world.

It may be that the hour I had at Gethsemani is the core religious experience of the animist life. What I mean is that this experience is sufficient to account for the existence of animism as a world religion. I'm not saying this well. . . . I'll put it this way: Anyone who has this experience is an animist from that moment on. Anyone who has this experience knows that the world is ablaze with divine life, and that's the center of the animist vision. I don't imagine that the tree out there "has a spirit in it."

What I know is that that tree is ablaze with divine life—
which isn't the same thing at all. I don't need to see that
fire again to know this. I've already seen it. An hour's
sight of it is enough for a lifetime.

Animism is the only world religion that doesn't need to
scurry to get aboard the environmentalist bandwagon. It
was there long, long before the bandwagon started rolling
among the Takers. . . .

Are the others scurrying? Oh, yes, I'd say so. A couple
years ago, Carl Sagan produced an article for *Parade* mag-
azine in which spokespersons for all the major religions
(not including animism, of course) declared that they'd
"always" been environmentalist in some sense or other.
I'll do the gentlemanly thing and suggest that perhaps
they're out of touch with their
own historical roots. All the
major world religions (always
excluding animism, of course),
are founded on these notions:
that man and man alone was
the desired object of creation,
that man occupies a preemi-
nent place in the order of creation, that man has a value in
God's eyes that is transcendently greater than that of all
other creatures, that this world of matter is illusory, tran-
sitory, and worthless.

> *Animism is the only
> world religion that
> doesn't need to
> scurry to get aboard
> the environmentalist
> bandwagon.*

Of them all, Judaism is the least otherworldly. Its mystical tradition recognizes the need to "leave room"—for
one's spouse, for one's children, and, by easy extension,
for all living creatures. Of them all, Christianity is the

most insistently man-centered. God did not give his only-begotten son for anything in the world but the people in it. Christ very definitely did not come to save the whales.

John the evangelist summarizes the Christian view very succinctly: "Anyone who loves the world is a stranger to the Father's love," and of course, "The whole world lies in the power of the evil one." I don't doubt for a moment that there are many in this tradition who would say this is exactly what I experienced that day at Gethsemani: the power of the evil one.

The "majors" have no authentic message of their own concerning the degradation of our environment, the diminishment of biological diversity, the destruction of the creative processes that brought forth and sustain life on this planet, the end of speciation (which, to the mind of the animist, is creation itself), the extinction of species —even of our own species. These concepts are simply not in their theological vocabulary. Why should they be? From their very foundation, these religions were about making people holy, were about uniting mankind with a god unthinkably remote from the sordid moil and muddle of mere biological survival. They can rewrite their prophets' lines to give them an environmentalist spin, but I frankly doubt that this will save them. Their irrelevance in the contemporary world is not one of appearance; it goes right down to the bone.

THIRTEEN

As I pointed out in *Ishmael,* we Takers are a desperately lost and needy people. It was this neediness, I think, that first made us yearn to be loved by God (an idea completely foreign to the animist mentality) and that made us dream of eternities of bliss after lifetimes of emptiness. If anything, our sense of neediness has grown even more overwhelming in recent decades. In addition to needing to be loved by God and to save our souls, we nowadays need to deepen our spiritual awareness, to raise our consciousness, to wield supernatural powers, to bend spoons with our minds, to grow our brains, to enhance our performance, to draw on the right side, to believe in the value of our creativity, to become more cosmic, to learn to fly, to investigate past lives, to have out-of-body experiences, to achieve lucid dreaming, to learn healing massage, to amplify our archetypes, to make our fantasies concrete, to explore our myths, to get rid of toxic introjects, to find our personal sacred site, to heal our inner child, to improve our experiential focusing, to be rebirthed, to take part in intrapsychic activities, to have a primal, to engage in cognitive restructuring, to indulge in cosmic play, to tune in to the godhead, to spend time on the astral plane, to have an intuition workout, to enhance our ch'i, to contact our spirit guide, to tap into the hypnagogic state, to increase our thanatological awareness, to have a soul reading, to visit a sacred energy vortex—and this hardly scratches the surface. Don't think I'm making fun of these things just because I put them into a list; to the people who engage in them, these are all as real and important as achieving nirvana or saving one's soul.

The neediness of the Takers is so immense that many people imagine that this neediness is *itself* the problem that is threatening the world. I've actually had heated arguments with people who insist that one or another or some combination of the above is all that is needed to save the world or that saving the world can only be accomplished by one or another or some combination of the above or that one or another or some combination of the above is an absolutely essential prerequisite to saving the world.

The sun is at the horizon. It's time for us to finish.

If nothing else, I hope you'll carry this idea away with

you: Attend to your needs, but don't confuse attending to your needs with saving the world.

There was a time when I thought I could say to people: "Forget yourselves for a while, because the world is in dire need of your attention. For a while stop looking for ways to enhance your inner life and start looking instead for ways to ensure that—twenty years from now, fifty years from now—our children and grandchildren will have a decent world to grow up in." I'll still say it, but now I say it knowing that this is too much to ask of most people.

It doesn't matter, I'll ask it of a few.

I hope the things I've given you here will enrich you as a person, but I hope you see that I haven't given them to you solely for your personal enrichment.

> *What the beetle said to me was: "You're needed there." You, too, are needed there.*

Following the deer into the forest was an immensely enriching experience for me, but I wasn't called to it so that I could be enriched. The beetle didn't say, "What you need is there." What the beetle said was: "You're needed there."

You, too, are needed there. I mean you who broke into my house in the middle of the night to talk to me. But I also mean you who hear these words. I mean you who will someday read these words. On this I don't hesitate to ask you to believe.

Believe me, you're needed there.

———

The secret they wanted to impart to me was not a secret until we made it one. It was known to the first of our kind to tread the face of the earth. It was known to every generation thereafter and never doubted, until we began to doubt it, some ten thousand years ago.

We're not strangers in a strange land here. This is the secret I learned. We're not aliens, not outsiders. We were born in the sea, three billion years ago. The deer and the beetle are our kin.

We're not invaders from space. No one gave us this planet to take care of or to use as we please. We grew out of the community of life the same way shellfish did, the same way mosquitos did.

The world doesn't belong to us, we belong to it. Always have, always will.

We belong to the world. We belong to the community of life on this planet—it doesn't belong to us. We got confused about that, now it's time to set the record straight.

We belong to the world, and this is why we're needed. No species can set itself apart from all the rest or make itself the ruler of all the rest. That won't work. All must belong.

That's what we've got to work on. We've got to find our way back into the community. We've got to stop living like outlaws. When we begin to do that—when we begin to acknowledge that the world needs us and that we belong to it, not it to us—I think our feelings of desperate loneliness and neediness will begin to evaporate, all by themselves.

I think maybe needy people are just people who don't feel needed.

Well, I say to you: Feel needed.

Feel needed, because you are.

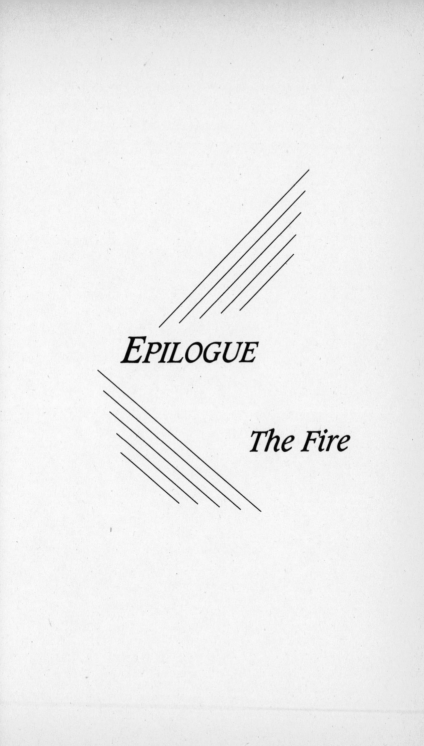

EPILOGUE

The Fire

This exaltation, paean, or anthem (my vocabulary—restricted as it is to Taker recognitions—provides no exact term for such an object) was written in about 1982. It represents a fusion of the insight that overtook me in the hills of Kentucky in 1954 with the understanding I subsequently gained of the animist vision of the universe. I didn't deliberately refrain from addressing it to any divine being. Only later did I recognize this aspect of it as an authentic expression of the animist sensibility.

of universes, the fire burns forever. It is the flame of life that courses through all generations from first to last, that burns without consuming, that is itself consumed and renewed inexhaustibly, life after life, generation after generation, species after species, galaxy after galaxy, universe after universe, each sharing in the blaze for its season and going down to death while the fire burns on undiminished. The fire is life itself, the life of this universe, of this galaxy, of this planet, of this place and every place: the place by the rock and the place under the hill and the place by the river and the place in the forest, no two alike anywhere. And the life of every place is god, who is the fire: the life of the pond, god; the life of the tundra, god; the life of the sea, god; the life of the land, god; the life of the earth, god; the life of the universe, god: in every place unique, as the life of every place is unique, and in every place the same, as the fire that burns is everywhere

/// *THE FIRE OF LIFE.* ///

ABOUT THE AUTHOR

DANIEL QUINN is the author of *Ishmael*. He is at work on a new novel, *The Story of B,* that continues the intellectual and spiritual journey begun in *Ishmael*.